Julia Kristeva

T0366699

Modern European Thinkers

Series Editors: Anne Beech and David Castle

Over the past few decades, Anglo-American social science and humanities have experienced an unprecedented interrogation, revision and strengthening of their methodologies and theoretical underpinnings through the influence of highly innovative scholarship from continental Europe. In the fields of philosophy, post-structuralism, psychoanalysis, critical theory and beyond, the works of a succession of pioneering writers have had revolutionary effects on Anglo-American academia. However, much of this work is extremely challenging, and some is hard or impossible to obtain in English translation. This series provides clear and concise introductions to the ideas and work of key European thinkers.

As well as being comprehensive, accessible introductory texts, the titles in the 'Modern European Thinkers' series retain Pluto's characteristic radical political slant, and critically evaluate leading theorists in terms of their contribution to genuinely radical and progressive intellectual endeavour. And while the series does explore the leading lights, it also looks beyond the big names that have dominated theoretical debates to highlight the contribution of extremely important but less well-known figures.

Also available:

Hannah Arendt
Finn Bowring

Alain Badiou
Jason Barker

Georges Bataille
Benjamin Noys

Jean Baudrillard
Mike Gane

Walter Benjamin
Esther Leslie

Pierre Bourdieu
Jeremy F. Lane

Gilles Deleuze
John Marks

André Gorz
Conrad Lodziak and Jeremy Tatman

Félix Guattari
Gary Genosko

Jürgen Habermas
Luke Goode

Jacques Lacan
Martin Murray

Bruno Latour
Graham Harman

Herbert Marcuse
Malcolm Miles

Guy Hocquenghem
Bill Marshall

Slavoj Žižek
Ian Parker

Julia Kristeva

Speaking the Unspeakable

Anne-Marie Smith

First published 1998 by Pluto Press
345 Archway Road, London N6 5AA

www.plutobooks.com

British Library Cataloguing in Publication Data
A catalogue record for this book is available from the British Library

ISBN 978 0 7453 1058 9 Hardback
ISBN 978 0 7453 1057 2 Paperback

Typeset by Stanford DTP Services, Northampton, England
Printed and bound by CPI Group (UK) Ltd, Croydon, CR0 4YY

Contents

Acknowledgements   vi

Abbreviations   vii

Introduction   1

1. The Semiotic and the Symbolic   14

2. The Abject, the Maternal and Melancholy   30

3. Transference, Time, Literary Experience   49

4. Foreignness, Femininity, Sacrifice   77

Conclusion   95

Notes   98

Bibliography   103

Index   107

Acknowledgements

This book is dedicated to my daughters Elena and Laura.

I would like to express my thanks to Keith Reader, who first put me in contact with Anne Beech at Pluto Press, and to Anne Beech herself for her patience and support, and for reading the manuscript in its later stages. For helping me reflect upon Kristeva's place in Anglo-American critical thought I owe thanks to those colleagues who participated in the Kristeva symposium I organised in London in 1996: Judith Still, Margaret Atack, Anna Smith and Jonathan Rée. I would also like to thank my daughters' grandparents for important holiday childcare.

In France, I owe thanks to Julia Kristeva herself who has been open to dialogue at all stages of this book and whose seminar at Paris VII is a source of vitality and inspiration; and to many unnamed friends, and colleagues at Paris VIII, for discussion and encouragement. I would like to thank my husband Stephen Di Biasio for his accompaniment across frontiers.

And thanks also to M.F.

Anne-Marie Smith

Abbreviations

Lrlp	*La révolution du langage poétique*
Pdh	*Pouvoirs de l'horreur*
Enm	*Etrangers à nous-mêmes*
Hd'a	*Histoires d'amour*
Sn	*Soleil noir*
Lnma	*Les nouvelles maladies de l'âme*
Lts	*Le temps sensible*
Snsr	*Sens et non-sens de la révolte*

Julia Kristeva

Introduction

I am one of those who think that in spite of the technical era in which we live ... there exists a life of the psyche which to me is still the essential value of our civilisation. It is not limited to the individual but, through subjective experience, situates man in history and beyond the history of events, in the monumental history of Being.

To those preoccupied with the renewing of tradition I say that I consider it crucial to maintain the tradition of revolt. Alongside a culture of complacency, a culture of entertainment, a show-culture, Europe and its peoples are the depositary of a culture of revolt. This is revolt in the etymological sense of the word, which also means 'research' in the Proustian sense of the word, that is, in the sense of return, displacement or contestation.

Je suis de ceux qui pensent que, malgré l'ère technique dans laquelle nous vivons ... il existe une vie psychique qui me paraît toujours être la valeur essentielle de notre civilisation. Elle n'est pas limitée à la personne mais, à travers l'expérience subjective, situe l'homme dans l'histoire et, par delà l'histoire événementielle, dans l'histoire monumentale de l'Etre.[1]

A ceux qui se soucient de renouer avec la tradition, je dirai qu'il me paraît indispensable de maintenir la tradition de révolte. A côté d'une culture de complaisance, de divertissement et de 'show', les peuples européens sont les dépositaires d'une culture révolte. Au sens étymologique du mot 'révolte', qui est aussi le sens de la 'recherche' selon Proust: retour, déplacement, contestation.[2]

Julia Kristeva arrived in Paris from her native Bulgaria at the age of 25 in the winter of 1966, armed with a doctoral fellowship and a small suitcase. She is now an intellectual figure of international renown, a psychoanalyst, writer and literary critic whose work takes place against the background of a French intellectual tradition from which it stands out and speaks in a dissident, interrogative voice which guarantees its potential for other contexts, cultures and disciplines. Julia Kristeva presents her position in France as one which is ambivalent. She has adopted a country which despite its symbolic recognition of her work – in January 1997 she was awarded the prestigious *légion d'honneur* – could never adopt her foreignness; France is a profoundly ethnocentric, phallocentric country, and foreignness, dissidence and femininity are integral factors in Julia Kristeva's construction of her intellectual identity. As exiles often do, she says she sometimes thinks of leaving, that there is a misogynist, xenophobic, Poujadist side to France, which she finds intolerable.[3] This seems to be more an expression of exile than the declaration of any purpose on Kristeva's part. Such expressions of exile evoke the love/hate passion generated by a 'double belonging' and highlight the paradox that when Kristeva leaves Paris, as she often does, for international engagements, outside France she is considered the quintessence of Frenchness, an absurdity which begs the question of cultural identity with insistent irony. The French language is the place from which she speaks and to which she returns, yet it is not her native language and Kristeva does not identify with the French intellectual tradition per se. She has always insisted upon the need for identity to be at once non-fixed and yet guaranteed, the need for dissidence and transgression to be contained within a structure. In this light, her own identification with

the French language as the place from which she speaks
and experiences what she speaks can be seen as a necessary
structure for her interrogation of the rigid codes and
practices which characterise the grammar of that language
and inform the French intellectual tradition.

Kristeva quickly became an important figure in the
Parisian intellectual scene of the late 1960s. She married
the novelist and critic Philippe Sollers who edited the
avant-garde literary journal *Tel Quel* and she was closely
involved with the *Tel Quel* group's activities for a number
of years. She and Sollers are still married and in the
summer of 1996 publicly celebrated the thirtieth
anniversary of their freely unfaithful and respectfully
independent union. Yet even in joint interviews with the
French magazine press Kristeva cuts a very different
profile to her husband. This need for distinction may in
fact explain her willingness to participate in the media
interest which surrounds her marriage. From the mid-1970s
onwards she has very much forged her own path. With
the publication of her brilliant doctoral thesis *La révolution
du langage poétique* in 1974 she secured a chair in linguistics
at the University of Paris VII where she still teaches. As
a university teacher she is engaged with the demands this
imposes on one's discourse in constant need of renewal
and dialogue through the encounter with students and other
academics. As both public intellectual and academic she
is forever involved in the practice of reviewing her own
place and situating her personal history both in a critical
and more general historical context. Becoming both a
mother and a psychoanalyst in the late 1970s certainly
brought a change in Kristeva's style. Her writing became
more fluid and accessible and during this period she
initiated an enquiry into the representation of the maternal,
and by extension the feminine, in culture, and into the
structural importance of the mother–infant relationship
which is still at the heart of her intellectual and psychoanalytic practice.

Kristeva's oeuvre now spans more than thirty years. Her
first French publication 'Le Mot, le dialogue, le roman'
('Word, Dialogue, Novel') appeared in the journal *Critique*
in 1967 and her seventeenth critical work, the second
volume of *Pouvoirs et limites de la psychanalyse* came out
in May 1997, by which time she had also completed three
novels.[4] There have been distinctive shifts in Kristeva's
critical interests during this time notably from linguistics,
structuralism, cultural analyses of the maternal and of racial
intolerance to an increasing focus on the importance of
psychoanalysis as the only human science capable of
restoring meaning to the lives of individuals in times of
distress such as those which define Western culture as it
reaches into the third millennium. Kristeva's personal
commitment to psychoanalytic practice and psychic health
is abundantly clear as are the brushstrokes this gives to
her biography, that as well as being a renowned intellectual
and teacher she is an analyst and as such is engaged in a
process of intimacy, an acceptance of exposure to personal
suffering, and unique forms of identification, distance
and interpretation which spill over into all one's practice.

During the past thirty years the innovative concepts for
which Kristeva became renowned and which she
formulated in her own vocabulary have evolved and
assumed new significance. Kristeva now adopts the classical
terms of psychoanalytic theory, submitting to a common
language, rather than forging her own. So her work has
become more fluid, open and accessible, and some critics
lament that the sharp edge of avant-gardism has been lost
to the synthesising power of Freudian psychoanalysis.[5] But
what is most striking about Kristeva's critical oeuvre,
apart from her sheer productivity, is its conceptual
coherence and the sense it produces of being a vast,
integrated work-in-progress of cultural critique.
Furthermore, given the way the evolution of her work
clearly represents her life we could say that Julia Kristeva
is an exemplary advocate of her own thinking, a living

example of its dynamism, complexity and conflicts, its powers of transgression within limits and remarkable capacity for synthesis.

There are many interpretations and readings of Julia Kristeva's work available in England and America. Toril Moi's *The Kristeva Reader* (1986) provides a clear analytic critique of Kristeva's key texts up to 1985. John Lechte's *Julia Kristeva* (1990) concentrates on Kristeva's place in French cultural and intellectual history and Anglo-American responses to this, including the author's own, especially with respect to 'horror', 'love' and 'melancholy', as a prescriptive reading. *Abjection, Melancholia and Love: The Work of Julia Kristeva* (1990), an interdisciplinary collection of essays, variously inspired by Kristeva's work, is symptomatic of the effect of her thinking upon contemporary Anglo-American critics working in Literature and the Human Sciences. Kelly Oliver in the United States has published readings of Kristeva from an American feminist standpoint. Anna Smith in New Zealand provides an original and compelling reading of a selection of texts in terms of exile and estrangement in her recent book.[6] Kristeva is no stranger to the debate which surrounds her work in an Anglo-American context. As well as occupying a chair, as visiting professor, at Columbia University, she is regularly translated by Leon Roudiez for Columbia University Press and has recently been translated by Stephen Bann in Britain. We might say that Kristeva has an Anglo-American identity, an identity she does not entirely own and which does not always seem to fit. There is a certain Anglophone representation of Kristeva, influenced by the feminist readings of Stone, Oliver and Jardine, which tends to characterise her conservatism, religiosity and lack of political edge or de-politisation. One cannot ignore issues of translation and cultural difference in the representation of a writer's thought. These questions inform my own enquiry which makes an issue of the specificity of the French language as well as going against the grain of recent representations in an attempt to reopen the debate in terms of my personal impressions of Julia Kristeva's work against the background of the French tradition. In this context I am struck by, and have chosen to emphasise, her free-thinking and thoughtful exorbitance, commitment to individual freedom, to psychic health and her insistent conviction in the sublimatory powers of cultural activity.

I have been attending Kristeva's seminar at Paris VII for some years and have heard her lecture in different intellectual contexts. I find myself constantly having to renew my idea of her identity and to account for that versatility and porosity which characterise her thinking. Yet at the same time I am overwhelmed with its coherence in the sense of a fidelity to itself, that capacity to integrate and renew thirty years' thinking with distance, irony and insight. It is rather like a mature adult looking back upon the doubts, convictions and conflicts of his youth and childhood with the sort of tolerance that enables him to integrate all the brushstrokes into a complex, differentiated picture.

My introduction to Kristeva's thought is written then from a particular perspective. It offers a close reading of Kristeva's texts, especially her most recent work. It is a reading of the French texts and as such is a work of translation and interpretation. In elaborating links with earlier texts it also provides a global picture of Kristeva as a living thinker who is constantly responding to and addressing the cultural environment of which she is a product. It aims to represent the evolution of that thought in both a diachronic and synchronic way, that is, in terms of chronological time, history and personal biography, and cyclical time – time which allows repetition and return, the time of personal history and subjectivity.

As such the approach itself is a representation of certain of Kristeva's key concepts: of identification as a key to understanding and elaborating meaning, of boundary crossing as a radical move in the creation and evolution of any form of identity, of time and history as necessarily both *cursive* – linear, and *monumental*, – cyclical and revolutionary in the Nietzchean and Kristevan sense. In a sense then this book is written from within, from within the framework of Kristeva's thought, from within a distinct French context, which is different and a long way from how I see the English and American critical purchase of Kristeva's work. Yet like Kristeva's work it is also written from outside that French context since the French language is neither her maternal tongue nor my own. But French is Kristeva's adopted language. She professes an energetic and exclusive attachment to the French language as the place where she constructs her meaning.[7] This fact cannot be overlooked and I have chosen to pay attention to and translate that specificity, of the French language, of Kristeva's text. In a sense I am making translation an issue and in so doing attempting to check and slow down the rapid British and American consumption and critique of Kristeva which is itself symptomatic of the vast cultural differences between Britain or America and France. Since it constantly wrestles with problems of identity and difference be they cultural, sexual or political, Kristeva's text itself provides the best responses to the questions and misinterpretations posed by her Anglo-American readers. Often these questions are a problem of translation and very often arise from the refusal to see or perhaps more legitimately the refusal to espouse Kristeva's commitment to an ethics of identity and difference which is clearly psychoanalytic and Freudian.

These are questions which travel along an axis from France across the Channel and the Atlantic and back again, and they represent cultural differences, such as the difference between Anglo-American and French psycho-analytic thought. I would argue that Kristeva is a committed Freudian in the French sense of the term and that Freud is certainly in a more comfortable position in France than

in Britain or the United States, where in the wake of the
recent vituperative indictment of Freud written by the
American intellectual Frederick Crews, the national,
liberal press has entered into a trend which, setting psychoanalysis against the demands of empiricism, attempts to
disprove its theories as non-scientific. The French Lacanian
tradition reads Freud as a study of language and Kristeva
must be situated firmly in this context. It is impossible to
comprehend the full import of her work if one leaves out
its Freudianism.

I am therefore concerned with proposing two
hermeneutic practices: close-reading and translation, and
Freudian psychoanalytic thought, as fundamental to a
proper understanding of Kristeva's work.

One of the aims of the Modern European Thinkers
series is to make continental philosophy more accessible
to a British and American readership and in so doing to
break through the intimidating frontiers of strangeness,
of distrust and yet fascination with 'things continental'.
The photograph on the cover of the paperback edition
symbolises that attempt to present the foreign as human
and accessible as it also encapsulates the lure of the image
and its seductive appeal. That in itself is a step in the
direction of the foreign. I think there is an aspect of French
cultural life in general which involves unabashed avowals
of desire and seduction and distinct forms of identification which a puritanical streak in Anglo-American culture
resists as narcissistic or uncritical and needs to turn into
either abstractions or plain speech. The book and the
manuscript are in France fetishistic objects, objects of
unashamed sensory appeal. Intellectuals and their public
participate with evident pleasure in the performance of the
seminar. Lacan is remembered for his theatrical dress
sense and especially his ties, Barthes for his seductive
voice. The attractiveness and unabashed sensual appeal
of certain women philosophers in France have often
disconcerted British and American feminists. Kristeva is

no exception. There is a staging of sensory pleasure which is not always considered politically correct, or critical, across the Channel or the Atlantic. This is a form of resistance which goes far beyond distinguishing the package from the product and in the name of critique translates itself as a refusal of seduction, and an obsessional defence against the hysteria of foreignness and femininity. This sort of defensiveness is of course at the basis of any serious critical work but it is also a measure of cultural difference which is played out, I would argue, in relation to the question of seduction and its resistance. All forms of appraisal, homage and critique can be measured in terms of seduction and resistance, just as xenophobia and misogyny are extreme examples of defences against the lure of foreignness or femininity. What I am trying to argue here is just as one cannot afford to economise Kristeva's Freudianism, nor can one afford to economise her foreignness or her femininity.

The fact that many French women philosophers such as Cixous, Irigaray and Kristeva are taken more seriously outside France than within, is consonant with the fact that French culture is more prone to sexism than to misogyny. French women intellectuals struggle for recognition from the male establishment but they do not have to struggle for recognition of their femininity. There are losses on both sides. Anglo-American women intellectuals are often pressurised to pay the price for their recognition from the male establishment in terms of their femininity and to become closet-women, closet-mothers. The French provision of generous maternity rights and highly-subsidised state childcare facilities is indicative of this difference, of the state supporting women to be working women and mothers, of the state's recognition of femininity. Kristeva is no stranger to this web of cultural difference and its evident intersections with sexual difference.

The debate Kristeva provokes among Anglo-American feminists can be seen in the light of such questions of cultural and sexual difference. In 1996 I organised a conference on Kristeva's work in which I invited Anglophone academics to discuss their encounter with Kristeva's oeuvre in terms of *Powers of Transgression*.[8] In this context Judith Still referred to what Anglo-American feminists see as Kristeva's conflation of the feminine and the maternal. She wondered whether Kelly Oliver's feminist arguments, such as the claim that Kristeva addresses the maternal in relation to the male child only, might be related to her misreading of the pronoun 'il' in Kristeva's text, reading the French generic or the translation of the French generic as standing for the male child only. In the same vein I myself wondered about the massive transference of cultural baggage involved in the English translation of the French 'féminin'. In English the term 'feminine' immediately assumes connotations of culturally-imposed gender difference and stands in opposition to feminist. In French the term describes quite simply and neutrally that which belongs to women – women's bodies, needs, clothes, bicycles, etc. Given that all men have had mothers, then they too have belonged to women, to a woman's body, they too are faced with integrating the feminine, and this difficulty is played out in sexual relationships and represented across literature and the arts. This is why Kristeva, after Freud, maintains that the feminine is what is difficult, if not impossible, for both sexes. This is why one cannot talk about femininity without addressing the maternal. It is not difficult to see how this fact has feminist hackles rising in Britain and the United States. Yet, significantly, French feminists do not problematise the feminine in the same way. Cixous and Irigaray, for example, are more concerned with the cultural importance of representing and imagining femininity in its inalienable difference than with arguing for parity. With her emphasis on the maternal Kristeva treads an ethical, non-separatist path which is fundamentally psychoanalytic and invites men

and women to negotiate the problem of femininity, to look
the mother in the face and assume their sexual identity.
She herself assigns some of the difficulty her text poses
for Anglo-American feminists to the differences between
a protestant or puritanical tradition, and European
catholicism in which the sacred cult of the Madonna
occupies an important symbolic and at best sublimatory
place and in which it is easier to address the question of
the maternal as a representation and an emotive, aesthetic
issue, than it is in a puritanical tradition which associates
the maternal with enclosure or domesticity. Indeed her
work illuminates these questions and I shall discuss cultural
and sexual difference in Kristeva's text in terms of
Foreignness and Femininity in the final chapter of this book.

Reading French philosophers such as Sartre, Lacan,
Barthes, Derrida, Cixous, Irigaray and Kristeva is a difficult
task and one might argue that the most interesting, most
liberal readings take place outside France. In France these
thinkers are very much part of a revolutionary, subversive
thread in French culture which takes place in the margins
of and yet is in a curious way fostered by the conformism,
centralism and archaisms of state-machinery and a
laborious Napoleonic educational system. So radical
thinkers and female intellectuals are both marginalised and
yet produced by a general culture characterised by
conservatism, classical rigour and profound ethnocentrism.

While being seen as the quintessence of French cultural
life outside France, Julia Kristeva reiterates her foreignness
time and again and indeed the centrality of foreignness
to her intellectual position. She is an exile who in her 1977
essay 'Un nouveau type d'intellectuel: le dissident' ('A New
type of Intellectual: The Dissident') related dissidence to
an insistent form of critical questioning. More recently,
in 'Les nouvelles maladies de l'âme', an interview with
Catherine Francblin published in *L'Infini* in 1993, she
related the fact of being a woman intellectual to the

personal integration of estrangement and most recently, in 'Bulgarie, ma souffrance', published in *L'Infini* in 1995, wrote about her own personal exile from Bulgaria, her country of origin, and her maternal language as a source of suffering. So while situating Julia Kristeva in a French context I shall also emphasise the structural importance of foreignness or strangeness in her thought and its relation to questions of identity, boundary-crossing, melancholy, and femininity.

Much of Kristeva's work is available in English. While giving bibliographical references to these translations I shall provide my own translations of the works selected for commentary. I have chosen to focus on specific later texts from 1979 onwards, yet beginning with and referring back to *La révolution du langage poétique* (*Lrlp*) (1974), her seminal work, the text from which all the others might be seen to emerge and to which they lead back. This text was Kristeva's doctoral thesis, and like the seminal work of many great thinkers it is dense, brilliant, often inaccessible, a Herculean trial she will never repeat, and yet which repeats itself. The later texts are more accessible, personal and open. There are obvious omissions in this selection, which corresponds to the attempt to provide a global picture which has a sense of chronology and interconnectedness and revolves around a series of key-concepts which provide the chapter titles, each chapter providing a close reading of extracts in French from key-texts which are cited with the chapter heading. It is hoped the reader will be able to see and interpret any Kristeva text in the context of the evolution of her thought traced in these chapters. I have chosen not to comment directly upon Kristeva's novels in this book. Their intersection with and independence from her intellectual production is interesting and important but can only receive indirect illumination from this particular study. Equally, Kristeva's involvement with the *Tel Quel* group and the group's participation in the events leading up to and from May 1968 has been recently documented both in Britain by Patrick Ffrench and in France by Philippe Forest and does not form part of the focus of this study.[9] My aim is to provide the reader with a theoretical frame of reference for his or her own intellectual projects and encounters with Kristeva's oeuvre.

CHAPTER 1

The Semiotic and the Symbolic

In 1974 Julia Kristeva published *La révolution du langage poétique,* the work in which she launched the key concepts of *the semiotic* and *the symbolic.* It is the most complex of Kristeva's texts and the exposition of these terms in that text provides a high-powered condensation of an attention to the realm of the sensible and its encounter with the laws of language which will evolve and be elaborated over the next thirty years and more. In this sense it is the most revolutionary of Kristeva's texts for the argument that poetic language points to the fact that language cannot live by grammar or syntax or even vocabulary alone, that sensation will leave its indelible stamp and that this imprint of the body in language is readable, will be returned to and opened up in all subsequent writing. The theory that language owes its vitality and capacity for renewal to this infiltration of subversive forces which rock the status quo also means that a culture is kept alive and owes its dynamism to artistic activity and an individual's health is bound up with her capacity to create and imagine. This theory provides the hallmark of Kristeva's personal contribution to thinking in literature and the arts. It accounts for the fact that she not only provides an inspiration for artistic practice as well as criticism but is also in demand at many international events in the artworld.

If I have chosen to trace the evolution of the concepts of the semiotic and the symbolic through Kristeva's work it is because I think that despite being loosely used in Anglo-American critical theory they have not received the sort of attention which reviews them in the context of Kristeva's work as a whole and still remain misunderstood by many.

In *La révolution du langage poétique*, Julia Kristeva espoused a Freudian theory of the subject and its origins, which is still at the basis of her most recent thinking. This theory of the speaking subject revolves around Kristeva's description of the symbolic and the semiotic as conceptual and dialectical categories. Before examining these categories it helps to see their derivation and difference from Lacan's model of the three interacting Symbolic, Imaginary and Real orders. For a clear detailed exposition of Lacan's three orders I refer the reader to *The Works of Jacques Lacan* by Bice Benvenuto and Roger Kennedy.[1] It is important to emphasise, with the authors of this study, that in the formulation of these three orders, Lacan places particular emphasis on the elaboration of the symbolic order which covers the whole area of the functions of speech and language.

In *Lrlp*, Kristeva departs from Lacan to elaborate the function and place of the pre-verbal semiotic and its manifestations in language and speech. John Lechte's *Julia Kristeva* offers a close reading of these categories in terms of the study of avant-garde poetic language which is the focus of Kristeva's preoccupation in this particular work.[2] What I am interested in showing is how the whole of Kristeva's oeuvre, and indeed the importance of her contribution to psychoanalytic and literary thought in particular, involves a consistent elaboration of the category of the semiotic and its interaction with the symbolic. Kristeva's semiotic, pre-verbal sign announces prosody, poetry's departure from prose, musicality and the unspeakable forces, energy and drives, which poets and artists strive to express in their attacks against and modifications of traditional forms; it announces the infancy of the child and of the child's relationship with the mother prior to language acquisition and symbolic separation. This is a phase of existence that psychoanalysis refers to as the pre-oedipal or as primary narcissism, a state of being which precedes the evolution of oedipal identity in the symbolic.

The semiotic can be seen as an articulation of unconscious processes which fracture the common idealisation of those images and signs which secure the status quo, and guarantee the establishment. It is a constant and subversive threat to the symbolic order of things, which itself, Kristeva stresses, is no monolithic structure, but an illusion of stability.

It might be argued that in *Lrlp* a Freudian model of language is already present since this work does not ignore the subject's relation to the body, and at the basis of the theory of the semiotic are the corporeal origins of any linguistic subject. The semiotic draws upon a sort of corporeal memory to which psychoanalysis commonly refers as 'mnemonic traces', a reminiscence of the play of energy and drives – both destructive and pleasurable – experienced in the body with great intensity before the achievement of real and symbolic separation from the mother, of subjectivity. The semiotic then is not this state itself, which corresponds to Lacan's order of the Real – death and 'jouissance', unspeakable destruction and unspeakable pleasure – but the memory, the inscription of this state in language. So the semiotic's transgression of and containment by the symbolic enables the impossible forces of the Real to enter the symbolic and the pain of becoming a subject, separate from the archaic mother and regulated by the exclusion of the oedipal structure, to be symbolised. Such therapeutic symbolisation as this can be seen to be at work in art, poetic practice, love and psychoanalysis since in so far as these are all coded practices they enable subjects to be at once transgressive and contained by the social order. Forming an identity involves a struggle with and recognition of the agent of this separation – the real or symbolic father, the phallus. Lacan refers to this identity-forming paternal intervention as the name of the father and Kristeva, in *Lrlp*, will refer to this as the symbolic instance of the law, and later from *Pouvoirs de l'horreur* (1979) she will use Freud's term for the symbolic father, the father of individual pre-history. The subject is a speaking subject, *l'être parlant*, and the very existence of a subject posits the existence of the oedipal triangle and of separation. So individual subjects are separate and they need to bridge the gap between their solitude and the social structures which might alleviate it, between the body as need, the imagination as desire and the social corpus. The gap is bridged by the kind of imaginative activity which has a place somewhere in the social structure:

> Ainsi placé comme un lieu dialectique entre le système symbolique et l'hétérogéneité pulsionnelle qui agit en le menaçant, l'art assume la loi socio-symbolique, en même temps qu'il démontre la possibilité de sa transgression: il articule l'économie pulsionnelle des sujets à un code socialement admissible. Nous disons que cette dialectique est la condition même de la jouissance et que c'est la poésie qui la représente à travers le système du langage.[3]

> Thus placed as a dialectical area between the symbolic system and the work of instinctual heterogeneity whose action puts this constantly under threat, art takes the place of the socio-symbolic law, at the same time that it exposes the possibility of its transgression: it articulates the instinctual economy of subjects while submitting them to a socially admissible code. We claim that this dialectic is the very condition of *jouissance* and that it is poetry which provides a representation of this across the system of language.

All imaginative practice, such as art, poetry, love and psychoanalysis, represents the individual subject's encounter with the law of the father, of the symbolic and of society, with imposed form and structure, as well as representing the imaginative attempts to battle with this frame of reference in the name of desire, subjectivity and the energy and drives they bring into play. So the revolution of *Lrlp* refers to this fluid, subversive work of semiotic, instinctual forces within the symbolic. Attention to semiotic modalities focuses reading upon *signifiance,* representation, or the signs of meaning – on the play of signifiers in a text which move through and beyond *signification* – literal meaning, or the relationship between the word and the thing. The semiotic, insists Kristeva, is not an extension of the language system but transversal to and coextensive with it. It is through the semiotic that we can connect language as a formal system to something outside this, in the realm of the psycho-somatic, to a body and a bodily subject structuring and de-structuring identity.

The semiotic is then a kind of pre-verbal energy at work in the text and Kristeva acknowledges that her theory bears a debt to Melanie Klein's work on the instinctual economy of infancy and the expression of the drives which the infant achieves pre-verbally in echolalia and vocalic and intonational differences. While Melanie Klein was most concerned with analysing the phantasmatic configurations the infant represents in play and especially in relation to the mother, Kristeva is concerned with the semiotic inscriptions of this in language in the symbolic. It is this particular concern which enables Kristeva to bridge linguistics, which we might consider her first area of research, with psychoanalysis and its focus upon the relation of sexuality to language. Indeed Kristeva moved empirically from linguistics to psychoanalysis via the child and a study of children's language acquisition which she carried out in the crèche of the university at Paris VII. In *Lrlp,* commentary upon children's language acquisition goes hand in hand with poetic analysis.[4]

It is important to stress that the semiotic and the symbolic are conceptual modalities which are always inseparable:

> Le sujet étant toujours sémiotique et symbolique, tout
> système signifiant qu'il produit ne peut être
> 'exclusivement' symbolique, mais il est obligatoire-
> ment marqué par une dette vis à vis de l'autre.[5]

> Since the subject is always both semiotic and symbolic,
> any signifying system he/she produces is never
> 'exclusively' symbolic, but necessarily marked by a
> debt to the other modality.

Artistic practice has a privileged relation to the semiotic.
Avant-garde art, for example, can be seen visibly to fracture
the totalising discourse of fixed perceptions in the symbolic
to produce a new art form which on the canvas represents
heterogeneous forms and breaks in structure. The artist
who is in contact with the chaos of the drives at their most
primitive and who strives to give them form shares a
privileged relation to the semiotic with the mother who
must educate the infant driven by bodily needs, and with
the psychoanalyst who provides a structure for the patient's
regression. We can associate the semiotic with the child's
pre-oedipal relationship with the mother and the symbolic
with the child's socialisation, with post-oedipal identity.
It is clear that outside language or representation the
semiotic is unavailable for comment and that non-verbal
signifying systems such as music and painting, which
might be thought of as exclusively semiotic, also have
recourse to symbolic coded structures in so far as they
inscribe themselves in a cultural framework and we have
to use language to talk about them.

In *Lrlp* Kristeva argues that the poetic language of
Mallarmé and Lautréamont represents a spectacular
explosion of traditional literary discourse. What such
linguistic transgression demonstrates to us is that a
revolution in poetic language points necessarily to a
revolution in subjectivity. The revolution in poetic language
is not only inseparable from subjectivity but also from the
political in so far as the activity of the cultural avant-

garde will affect all discourse and therefore infiltrate the political arena. Thus Kristeva refers to a phenomenon whereby avant-garde literature can be seen to produce a spectacular *éclatement du sujet* or explosion of subjectivity and of the ideological limits which surround that subjectivity. These ideological limits, be they related to the family, society, or the state are then thrown into question, prevented from becoming totalitarian and made ripe for renewal by the questioning and disturbance of the semiotic. Since *Lrlp*, Kristeva's focus, along with her elaboration of the concept of revolution, has become increasingly psychoanalytic and in *Le temps sensible*, her recent reading of Proust, she elaborates the etymology of revolution in a Freudian and Proustian context as both a return to and a re-engagement with the past. The *sensible* of the French title of the book inscribes the semiotic – the representation of sensory experience – in the Proustian, Freudian time of remembrance, *le temps sensible*. In her most recent critical work, *Sens et non-sens de la révolte*, the poetry of Rimbaud, Lautréamont and Mallarmé is related to the first phase of what she calls literature's encounter with the Impossible which is traced in the second half of the book, in relation to the concepts of the sensible and of revolt, through the literary figures of Aragon, Sartre and Barthes.

So we can associate the semiotic with the child's pre-verbal relationship with the mother's body, and the symbolic with language and separation. In the child's development we see a diachronic evolution from infancy to language acquisition in which semiotic processes are never left behind and operate synchronically across language and other manifestations of subjectivity. The drives, as represented in the instinctual energy of the developing child, are checked by biological and social constraints. They nevertheless permeate what Kristeva calls semiotisable material, such as voice and gesture, and faced with real constraints, enter into a subjective economy which can be perceived as processes of condensation and displacement. In the literary text these processes take the form of metaphor and metonymy. They represent the way in which the pre-verbal operates synchronically across the signifying system and such processes are particularly apparent in dream. Like dream, poetic language, given that it is defined by its infringement of the laws of grammar and prose, brings together the linguistic or symbolic – *signification*, and the pre-verbal or semiotic – *sens*. It is in fact the function of poetic language, the poetic function as defined by Jakobson, to operate a return or, in Kristeva's language, a *revolution* from *signification* to *sens*.

Since it concerns the structure of human relations the symbolic corresponds to a kind of moral code. It is an inter-subjective social product regulated by the constraints of biological and sexual differences and by generational and historical differences. The literary text is a perfect example of a symbolic product and this is an aspect of the text Kristeva refers to as the *phenotext*, which is to be distinguished from the *genotext* – the textual inscription of semiotic modalities. What interests Kristeva in *Lrlp* is to trace the dialectical processes whereby the individual subject moves from one modality to another in poetic language through breaks in syntax and semantic structure. So in the text the semiotic is defined as musical, anterior, enigmatic, mysterious and rhythmic. It corresponds to Mallarmé's *le mystère dans les lettres*, mystery in letters, which Mallarmé relates both to musicality and to the woman as an incarnation of that mystery.

Kristeva introduces into her formulation of the semiotic the concept of a non-expressive in the sense of non-verbal totality underlying language; a non-spatial, non-temporal receptacle of energy and drives which she calls the *chora*. The chora will be qualified as feminine in the sense that it precedes any formation of subjectivity and phallic identity. Such access to language and identity involves a symbolic break with the imaginary maternal continent

22 JULIA KRISTEVA

and it is this break Kristeva will refer to as the *thetic*. The child's first words incorporating gesture, the object and the voice are already *thetic* in the sense that they mark a break, a frontier, a passage into language. It is this separation of an object from the subject in language which gives rise to a semiotic fragment – a word – with metaphoric or metonymic value and to the speaking subject. The failure to produce this identity-forming break may engender psychosis. In poetic language, rhythm, rhyme, alliteration, onomatopoeia, tone, modulation and word-play are all manifestations of Kristeva's semiotic order. In psychoanalysis, unspeakable emotion which is unavailable to consciousness and therefore to verbalisation can manifest itself in tone, timbre, intonation, modulation of voice, and in tears, and is referred to as affect, a term much used by the French psychoanalyst André Green and which derives from the Latin *affectivus*, French *affectif*, that which relates to emotion, pleasure and pain. Green criticises Lacan for an emphasis on representation which tends to exclude affect, and for the over-abstract quality of his theorising. For Green, drives, which are the representatives of internal excitations born in the body, reach the mind and achieve expression in the interrelation of representation and affect. The work of affect becomes possible as emotion, translated into words or signs, and brings forward representations which have been subjected to an adequate degree of repression.

It is the mother who for the child, and metaphorically for culture at large, facilitates, enacts and embodies the passage between semiotic and symbolic modalities and the path to representation. In this way pregnancy itself marks a boundary between singularity and ethics and the birth of the child an entry from nature into culture and the order of language. The text of motherhood, like the avant-garde poetic text, is a dynamic in which the heterogeneous forces of the semiotic and the cultural structures of the symbolic are inextricably linked. The mother is a double figure embodying at once the unspeakable experience of maternal fusion and the bridge to speech, culture and separation. We could describe pregnancy as the embodiment of a pre-oedipal threat to the oedipal script. The mother is both threatening and ethical, since the child's capacity for separation depends on her footing in a world outside the maternal continent which is her secret. As soon as she is perceived as other and separate by the infant, as soon as the thetic break between subject and object clears the way for the threshold of language, then the mother becomes a signifier, a place for the condensation or displacement of semiotic fragments. The thetic break from fusion is repeated and played out in the *fort-da* game which Freud describes from observing his infant grandson throwing and retrieving a cotton-reel while verbally articulating absence – *fort* – and presence – *da* – in an attempt to mimic and control his mother's absence and reappearance, to symbolise and to establish some mastery over the anxiety generated by separation. The fort-da is a pulsional process of division and separation which Kristeva names *le rejet* and which governs the subject's submission to the laws and objective struggles of nature and society. *Le rejet* corresponds to the *fort*, the child's throwing away of the cotton-reel, which is the acknowledgement that his mother is missing.

Defining and naming a topography of the pre-verbal and its relation to linguistic expression and to identity is part of the striking originality of *Lrlp*. To summarise, Kristeva's thesis is that with Nerval, Lautréamont and Mallarmé, the transformation of poetic language at the end of the nineteenth century is fundamentally a practice in which the semiotic can be seen to tear at and transgress the syntactic stability and constructions of identity proper to the symbolic. Late nineteenth-century poetry presents us with an example of the semiotic at work in literature. One of the key questions raised and discussed in *Lrlp* is how the pulsional dynamics of avant-garde poetic language relate to subjectivity. For Kristeva the literary avant-garde is a representation of the dialectical condition of the subject in language. In this sense the *révolution* of the title can assume a literary-historical sense since literature which announces itself in the symbolic order is also a subversion of the symbolic in that it is a *mise-en-procès*, that is, both a processing and a trial of a *sujet-en-procès*, a subject-in-process, of subjectivity. Like any subject the subject-in-process of writing is a subjectivity in revolt against constraint and against the signifier which announces fixed identity. So the subject's quest for identity, in literature or outside it, propelled by the desire to situate subjectivity, brings into play a never-ending struggle between the social – the arena in which one can speak and be heard – and the need to speak one's singularity. In this revolutionary process we are at the centre of the most radical heterogeneity maintained as a struggle between semiotic and symbolic forces and represented as subjectivity in struggle, that is as desire in language. *Lrlp* is a highly theoretical elaboration of the concepts of the symbolic and the semiotic and their place in poetic language. I have traced the vocabulary and key-concepts of this elaboration as well as the interconnectedness of psychoanalytic and literary thought within this. This exposition provides a conceptual basis for Kristeva's further thinking on the abject, the maternal, melancholia, the theory of revolt, the sensible, and cultural and sexual identity.

Illustration of the Semiotic

Before moving from *Lrlp* to the place of the semiotic and the symbolic in Kristeva's theory of the abject as introduced in *Pouvoirs de l'horreur* (*Pdh*), I should like to consider the above conceptual categories in relation to a specific literary text. I shall refer to James Joyce's text 'The Dead'.[6]

I shall begin by citing some key-passages from Kristeva's writing on the semiotic:

Nous sommes, avec cette pratique, au lieu de l'hétérogénéité la plus radicale, maintenue comme lutte contre le signifiant mais nous sommes au même temps au lieu de la différenciation signifiante la plus subtile.[7]

We are at the place of a most radical heterogeneity maintained as a struggle against the signifier yet at the same time we are at the site of the most subtle differentiation of the signifier.

Le désir de rendre voix à la différence sexuelle, et en particulier à la position du sujet-femme dans le sens et dans la signification, conduit à une véritable insurrection contre le signifiant 'homo-généisant'.[8]

The desire to give voice to sexual difference, and in particular to the position of the female-subject in meaning and in signification, leads to a veritable insurrection against the homogenising signifier.

Cette utilisation particulière du langage suppose une capacité identificatoire avec l'autre, avec le monde, les sons, les odeurs, ainsi qu'avec l'autre sexe, comme on le voit quand le narrateur s'incarne dans des personnages féminins.[9]

Joyce's particular use of language assumes a capacity for identification with the other, with the world, with sounds, with smells, as well as with the opposite sex, as we see when the narrator is embodied in female characters.

These quotations show how the activity of the semiotic can be related to the differentiation of symbolic codes and in particular to the inscription of the feminine in the text.

In Joyce's text (1907) the poetic interaction of symbolic and semiotic modalities is readable. In this text the symbolic categories of time, generational and historical differences, living and dead, and space – geography, outside and inside, are traversed by semiotic modalities – music, voice, accent, colour. These semiotic modalities are in turn embodied in the person of Gretta and her nostalgic subjectivity, her femininity.

'The Dead' relates a dinner-party which takes place on the feast of the epiphany at the house of two spinster aunts as it has for many years. At the opening of the tale the guests are arriving and the sexes are separated, symbolically, by a staircase. The men's cloakroom is downstairs and the ladies' room upstairs. It is cold outside, snow is falling and as the door opens and closes the outside enters in, 'a cold, fragrant air', and the guests carry in snow on their boots. It is the story of Gabriel and his wife Gretta. As the only married couple at the party they occupy a symbolic position – which will become progressively opened up, differentiated and revealed in all its heterogeneity by the work of semiotic elements in the text. This process is embodied in a moment of revelation, a Joycean epiphany, when Gretta will appear on the stairway, half-way between the men's domain and the women's domain, as a symbolic embodiment of the semiotic, as mysterious, musical, anterior and enigmatic: 'What is a woman standing on the stairs in the shadow, listening to distant music, a symbol of?'[10]

John Huston's film of this text (1987)[11] elaborates these semiotic dimensions with great finesse and subtlety. The film makes visible the various shades of red hair-colour which both separate and join all the women in the text. The different shades of red draw attention to generational differences: the three young music students are red-haired, Gretta's hair is rich bronze, Aunt Kate's a vivid nut-colour turning grey and Aunt Julia's grey-white. So colour operates symbolically, as symbolic of generational difference. But it also operates semiotically in a repre-sentation of nostalgia traversing the boundaries of time and space, living and dead, and drawing together different textual elements, giving volume to the poetic dimension of the text. This poetic dimension of the text privileges sense over signification, and the release of affect or emotion, here in the form of regret and nostalgia, embodied in the person of Gretta. Just as through the women's hair-colour, described in the text and repeated in the film, there is a visible passage from rich autumnal colours to winter monochrome, there is in the film a slow, sensitive passage from sepia shades to monochrome. This is visible as the camera moves across pale orange gas-lamps, the women's dresses – the young women wear beige and Gretta cream – the sepia family photographs which the camera pans during Aunt Julia's song, to focus on the snow covered city of Dublin, the outside where in the black night 'snow is general all over Ireland'. The camera finally rests on the landscape we see in black and white at the end of the film stripped of all colour where the relief is masked by snow and where the living are confused with the dead.

Gretta on the stairway appears as an icon veiled in white, a Madonna figure. She remains momentarily unrecognisable to her husband, and becomes a tableau, an enigmatic representation of femininity. So as the camera freezes upon a figure about to come down the stairs and join her husband but whose glance is turned towards a room upstairs, the viewer's participation in the symbolic categories of time and space is deflected to contemplation of a figure lost in listening to the melody of a song which travels far beyond Dublin and the dinner-party to her childhood in the West of Ireland. Music is semiotic, it transgresses the coded discourse of the family gathering, the codes of time and generation, the ties of marriage. It represents Gretta's secret and her personal exile. She stands in the half-light and the panels on her skirt which are terracotta and salmon-pink appear as black and white, the passage from orange-red-browns to monochrome traced in the text and which the film renders visible as it makes audible the music of the text and the accents and inflexions of textual material. In this sense John Huston's film, as film in general at its best, is a perfect instrument for giving volume and meaning to the sensory appeal of the text's semiotic dimension within the symbolic frame of the film.

Evolution of the Semiotic

Kristeva will further her enquiry into semiotic and symbolic modalities in her study of the etymology and practice of revolt and revolution and their relation to literary and psychoanalytic practice both in *Pouvoirs de l'horreur* and in *Sens et non-sens de la révolte*, as she will elaborate questions of identity, exile, displacement, and boundary-crossing, particularly in their relation to the maternal and the feminine, in *Etrangers à nous-mêmes*, *Histoires d'amour* and *Les nouvelles maladies de l'âme (Lnma)*. In the later book *Sens et non-sens de la révolte* (1996), Kristeva returns to the slow, unfolding topographies of Freud's model of the mind and of language. She examines and elaborates the detail of Freud's formulations and their relation to his clinical practice, personal history and biography. Her pre-occupations remain the same – how might language represent the unrepresentable? – but their elaboration has become more patient, more didactic, more supple. I shall return to this particular text at the end of Chapter 3.

It is in *Le temps sensible* that Kristeva will give the theory of the semiotic its fullest literary elaboration. In this book literary activity is seen as a dark-room in which sensory experience can be slowly processed, seen and understood in the wider context of interpersonal experience. The dark-room is also a motif for the sensibilisation and processing which takes place in a psychoanalysis and an antidote to what Kristeva sees as a crisis in contemporary subjectivity. This is very much the preoccupation of *Lnma*, a book in which Kristeva can be seen as a clinician treating symptoms of malaise in contemporary culture.

In *Pouvoirs de l'horreur* we can see how the transgressive process of revolt traced in *Lrlp* is developed into a theory of the revolt or disgust of the abject subject. The abject subject is the speaking subject in revolt against oedipal identity and sexual specificity. Abjection can be experienced as disgust which is a bodily form of revolt or as a phobic reaction against the polarised experiences of fusion and separation. Total revolt is impossible and this impossibility is the very condition of abjection. The theory of the abject accounts for the subject's difficulty in ever fully relinquishing the return to the archaic mother, represented in pre-symbolic, semiotic expression, for we revolt against the frontiers and boundaries which separate us from that maternal continent. Separation difficulty and abjection as a form of melancholy are therefore closely related. Abjection might be seen as a kind of transitional melancholy between the maternal continent and identification with the father in the symbolic. As such, the abject is closely bound up with questions of identity, boundary crossing, exile and displacement:

> Celui par lequel l'abject existe est donc un jeté qui (se) place, (se) sépare, (se) situe et donc erre, au lieu de se reconnaître, de désirer, d'appartenir ou de refuser.[12]

> (S)he through whom the abject exists is therefore an outcast who finds her place, makes a separation, situates herself and so wanders, instead of recognising who she is, and desiring, belonging or refusing.

In religious discourse forms of exclusion, transgression and taboo define the limits which lead to abjection and in so doing open access to the notion of the sacred which has a sublimatory function. According to Kristeva modern literature takes the sacred out of sublimation. Artistic experience which expresses and purifies the abject is thereby an essential component of religiosity. So reading Dostoevsky, Proust and Joyce we find a close correlation between literary expression of the abject and symbolisation of the maternal body. In this sense the maternal body is semiotic and the subject's return to and symbolisation of the maternal in artistic practice amounts to a sublimation of abjection.

CHAPTER 2

The Abject, the Maternal and Melancholy

In Kristeva's writings in the 1970s femininity is not designated as a sexually specific category, rather, through the theorisation of the semiotic, as a dimension of language available to either sex. While she consistently insists upon the importance of inscribing female identity and therefore womanhood within the constraints and frustrations of the symbolic order it is not until later, and with her increasing involvement in psychoanalytic practice, that Kristeva will elaborate in detail the specificity and difficulties of female identity. It is the focus on motherhood, which begins in *Pouvoirs de l'horreur* (*Pdh*) and extends into the writings of the 1980s, which provides the bridge between the linguistic categories of *Lrlp* and a more concrete clinical and critical engagement with real women such as is manifest in *Les nouvelles maladies de l'âme* (*Lnma*), *Sens et non-sens de la révolte* (*Snsr*) and, more recently, *La révolte intime*.

The focus on motherhood in writings of the late 1970s takes the form of the elaboration of a maternal ethic. This is the subject of Kristeva's essay 'Héréthique de l'amour' published in *Tel Quel* in 1977 and reprinted as 'Stabat Mater' in *Histoires d'amour* in 1983. In this essay the maternal ethic can be seen, in terms of the semiotic and the symbolic, as 'the semiotisation of the symbolic'. Poised at the limits of being and of language, the mother is at once a guarantee of the social order and a threat to its stability, a split subject which Kristeva represents in the text of 'Stabat Mater'. In this text a lyrical piece about her own pregnancy and birth-giving is juxtaposed with the theoretical text. Silence and repression weigh heavily upon the experience of motherhood and this text attempts a twofold expression of the maternal experience along the axis of semiotic and symbolic which divides the printed page. The left-hand side of the page verbalises the repressed maternal experience which will always be present as a layer of psychic identity, as an experience every mother and infant has shared:

On n'accouche pas dans la douleur, on accouche la douleur: l'enfant la représente et elle s'installe désormais, permanente.[1]

It is not a question of giving birth in pain but of giving birth to pain, the child represents that pain which will hitherto occupy a permanent place.

Nous vivons sur cette frontière, êtres de carrefour, êtres de croix. Une femme n'est ni nomade, ni corps mâle ... Une mère est un partage permanent, une division de la chair même. Et par conséquent, une division du langage – depuis toujours.[2]

We, creatures at the crossroads, creatures of the cross, are living on that frontier. A woman is neither a nomad, nor a male body ... A mother has always been a permanent division, a division of the flesh itself, and consequently a division in language.

Il y a ensuite cet autre abîme qui s'ouvre entre ce corps et ce qui a été son dedans: il y a l'abîme entre la mère et l'enfant ... Essayer de penser cet abîme: hallucinant vertige. Aucune identité n'y tient.[3]

There is then that other abyss between my body and what has been inside it: there is the abyss between the child and the mother ... Trying to imagine that abyss is as hallucinatory as it is vertiginous. No identity holds there.

These quotations point to an attempt to verbalise the pre-oedipal experience of the mother, that is the experience of blissful fusion with the infant child which will be symbolically interrupted, and according to the mother's desire, by a real or symbolic father-figure, as it is in fact always already. In the psyche such a state corresponds to an imaginary realm in which separation has not yet achieved any form of representation and can only then be fantasised as an abyss. The non-verbal exchanges of the imaginary pre-oedipal realm are an aspect of relationships between women which reproduce moments of fusional bliss and sensual exchange. In this sense, femininity, in the French sense of a state belonging to women, is the representation of an archaic maternal memory which corresponds to Kristeva's semiotic:

> Les femmes reproduisent sans doute entre elles, la gamme étrange du corps à corps avec leur mère. Complicité dans le non-dit, connivence de l'indicible du clin d'oeil, d'un ton de la voix, du geste, d'une teinte, d'une odeur: nous sommes là-dedans, échappées de nos cartes d'identité et de nos noms, dans un océan de précision, une informatique de l'innommable.[4]

> Women no doubt reproduce between themselves the strange gamut of forgotten corporeal fusion with the mother: tacit complicity, the unutterable connivance of a wink, a tone of voice, a gesture, a colour, a smell: we are there inside, stranded from our identity cards and our names in an ocean of precision, a code of the unnameable.

Pouvoirs de l'horreur examines the compelling power of archaic images – imagos – of the pre-oedipal mother in terms of the boundary state of abjection. Abjection lies between the pre-verbal infancy we associate with the imaginary and access to language, identification and the fixed forms of the objective world. The abject – *abjet* – as it is defined here might be related to the *rejet* of *La révolution du langage poétique*, the *rejet* being the child's libidinal separation from the mother, throwing the cotton-reel out of the cot in the *fort-da* game. The abject arises as a reaction when the individual comes up against all the barriers and limits which in society and culture define separation from the archaic mother. The individual reacts with horror, a mixture of revolt against the limits imposed and fear at the reminder of the forbidden realm of fusion, the maternal continent. Kristeva's classic example in *Pdh* is the revulsion experienced at the confusion of contact/separation, outside/inside when one's lips come into contact with the skin of milk. The beauty of this example is that, avoiding abstraction, it relates the abject to the body and in so doing illustrates the power and importance of visceral reaction as a representation of what is happening in the psyche. In the same way, the visceral feelings experienced in a dream are a key to the meaning of its narrative. We can link the experience of abjection to the child's first efforts at separation from the maternal body, to the attempt to distinguish and separate subject and object, and the depression which accompanies this process. Neither subject nor object, the abject lies between the two.

Evolution of the Abject

In his book *Julia Kristeva*, John Lechte provides an excellent close reading of Kristeva's theory of the abject and its evolution in writings on love and melancholy.[5] His interpretation might be summarised as follows: as the mother is a threat to boundaries – standing as she does for their effacement – rituals, in reinforcing identities, at the same time reinforce separation: that is, the existence of subject and object. Religious and cultural rituals enact symbolic separation from the maternal body. The abject is not a product of separation, rather a product of the organic drive for separation which will be experienced against the background of the experience of fusion and non-differentiation. In effect, the abject is not controlled by the (symbolic) law, but by the energy drives that in the end, are the condition of its possibility. The individual may come to terms with the responsibility and guilt generated by separation through speech, that is language which represents his imperfect participation in the human. In this sense the *felix culpa* – speaking sin – of Christianity is religion's missed opportunity for speaking the abject therapeutically.

In modern society, according to Kristeva, it is the artist, the writer and the analyst who embody the therapeutic possibility of speaking abjection. Lechte underlines the importance of Kristeva's essay 'L'abjet d'amour' printed in *Tel Quel* in 1982 and reprinted in *Histoires d'amour* as 'Freud et l'amour: le malaise dans le cure', stressing that the very title of the essay, 'The abject of love', evokes the movement away from the (abject) mother towards the (ideal) father. This very movement is the precondition for idealisation which forms the basis of love as agape (love tending towards the ideal) engaged in a neverending struggle with eros (passionate and destructive love).

That Kristeva has tended to identify *eros* with the mother and *agape* with the father in extreme polarisation is the subject of Anna Smith's study of Kristeva's novel *Le viel homme et les loups* (1990) – Kristeva's imaginary inquest into the death of her father which takes the form of a search for truth against a background of criminality and loss of meaning. Commenting upon a spatial and ethical distance between male *agape* and female embodiedness, Anna Smith provides a critique of the novel's polarisation of parental structures and argues that this is too extreme a distinction. She suggests that the heroine of this novel would not be so violently subject to estrangement and alienation if she could recognise 'her father as being in his body for her mother'.[6] I am not sure Kristeva adheres to this distinction as violently as the heroine of her novel does in Anna Smith's reading. It is certainly fundamental to her theory of psychic development that the mother should represent language as well as representing the body. Yet it is true that the theory of the 'abject of love' makes the symbolic distinction between maternal love as passionate and destructive and paternal love tending towards the ideal. The distinction is fundamentally symbolic. It is this symbolic break which characterises a child's exit from the Oedipus complex and acceptance of the law. I would argue that the father's love in this model needs to be seen as a sublimation rather than as something abstract and disincarnate since a sublimation is not an evacuation of eroticism, rather an acceptance of eroticism at a different, a more civilised, cultivated, level of experience.

Kristeva's writings on horror, love and melancholy have certainly provoked much debate in Britain and America. In 1990 Routledge published the proceedings of a Kristeva conference held at the University of Warwick in 1987. The title of the book, *Abjection, Melancholia and Love*, obviously refers to three of Kristeva's texts most recent to the conference: *Pouvoirs de l'horreur* (1980), *Histoires d'amour* (1983), *Soleil noir, dépression et mélancolie* (1987), and in this collection it is the theory of abjection which seems to provoke the most critical response.[7] Other key factors which emerge are what some critics see as the problematic status of Kristeva's theory of femininity, and its relation to writing on the maternal. In an essay called 'The Body of Signification', Elizabeth Gross, while pointing to the strength and originality of Kristeva's theory of abjection with its emphasis on the impossibility of the subject's revolt against biology and sexual difference, argues that Kristeva's emphasis on the paradigmatic mother–child relation with the mother as a bridge between nature and culture, grants no autonomy to female sexuality or femininity.[8] What Gross is really arguing with here is with the psychoanalytic structure of Kristeva's thinking and in fact with the oedipal structure in which sexual identity will always be submitted to the constraints of the oedipal triangle. When Gross criticises Kristeva for presenting maternity as a process without a subject, governed by the laws of biology, in effect as essentialist, and for not making sufficient distinction between the boy-child's and girl-child's exit from the Oedipus complex, she is making a feminist critique of Freudian psychoanalytic thought often repeated by American feminists talking about Kristeva's work. The finer points of Gross's argument are interesting. She seems to be saying that Kristeva is divided between the non-specificity which characterises abjection and which is the subject of much of her writing about poetic language, by men, and a kind of idealisation which characterises her analyses of religious discourse, that is, that she is divided between the (abject) mother and the (ideal) father, and that these polarities leave a gap for a more specific discourse about women's sexual and intellectual identity. This is an interesting argument which may have some historical truth but Kristeva has recently concentrated on a detailed elaboration of female sexual identity. In these recent writings she reflects upon Freud's reference to the dark inaccessibility of female sexuality and his evocation of the pre-oedipal mother–daughter relationship, epitomised in the well-known evocation of female sexuality as something as long concealed as 'the Minoan-Mycenaean civilisation behind the civilisation of Greece'. These issues will form the focus of my thinking in Chapter 4, 'Foreignness, Femininity, Sacrifice'. Moreover, reflections on foreignness and femininity inform Kristeva's present teaching, embodied in the figure of Hannah Arendt. Through Hannah Arendt Kristeva insists that the intellectual's role in politics passes through her imagination of a place for women and foreigners and thus she makes a close link between femininity and political imagination.

The most radical critique of Kristeva's theories of sexual difference seems to point to a polarisation of maternal and paternal identities which, as we have seen in relation to abjection, informs the Kristevan topography. In an essay in the volume cited above, entitled 'The An-arche of Psychotherapy', Noreen O'Connor repeats Gross's contention that Kristeva remains fixed upon a normative model of sexuality, a heterosexual model, and that this in turn signifies a difficulty in separating from the symbolic father.[9] One really has to see such readings of Kristeva, as more or less indicative of a critical ideology which is uncomfortable with the established rules of sexual difference in classical psychoanalysis. O'Connor, as her title suggests, tries to defend a form of psychotherapy in which sexual identity might be conceived as fluid and non-fixed. This is distinctly at odds with classical psychoanalysis and certainly contravenes Kristeva's argument that the end of psychoanalysis brings a choice of sexual identity even if that identity may be moderated by a playful knowledge of one's personal desires and secrets. In short, to argue that Kristeva is suffering from too close an identification with the symbolic father is a manner of defining oneself as a separatist feminist arguing with psychoanalytic thought. It is in any case certainly symbolic of the critic's own positioning before the symbolic limits of the oedipal structure and of paternity. The symbolic father is the sign of separation, the sign of the daughter's recognition of sexual difference, of generational difference, of the law against incest and the laws of heterogeneity which govern desire. This does not mean that female homosexuality, for example, stands to be irrevocably repressed by the law of the father. The laws of generational and sexual difference must be seen as a loose set of rules which individuals may use as borders while remaining free to live out their homosexuality on displaced or subliminal levels. Kristeva's reply to O'Connor's kind of critique would be to argue female homosexuality as an endogenous layer of female sexuality but one which might be sufficiently repressed, sublimated or traversed, a psychical bisexuality which forms part of the subject's quest for identity. That this psychical bisexuality is an integral part of femininity forms the substance of Kristeva's chapter on female identity in the first volume of *Pouvoirs et limites de la psychanalyse*.

I think Kristeva might share Freud's argument in seeing sublimated homosexuality as a great source of creative genius. This is part of Freud's thinking in his study of Leonardo da Vinci whose paintings of the Madonna and child can be seen to represent a sublimation of male homosexuality in which the painter's desire surrounds the infant-boy idealising the mother.[10] In the same way Kristeva's book on Proust will link the richness and diversity of Proust's representations to the writer's access to and partial sublimation of the complex layers of his own sexuality. She is concerned in showing how the precariousness of the subject's position in the symbolic, that is, the struggle with the symbolic father, is a source of revolt which finds its most intense and salutary form of expression in artistic practice. We can see how in Kristeva's thought literature and art, imaginary activity with some form of cultural or social – that is, symbolic – recognition, occupies a transitional and revolutionary space between abjection or confusion with the mother's body and too rigid an identification with the symbolic father – or totalitarianism.

In the essay in *Abjection, Melancholia and Love* entitled 'Horror, love and melancholy', John Lechte reads Kristeva's texts of the 1980s as a psychoanalytic attempt to enlarge imaginary and symbolic capacities, that is, to suggest, through the media of art and analysis, codes for representing the unnameable. I see Kristeva's preoccupation with the verbalisation of unspoken experience as a radical thread running through all her work. Her formulations of the semiotic, the abject, of melancholia, and of sense and the sensible are the conceptual and historical markers of her elaboration of this theme. It is moreover this question –

how unspoken experience may and does achieve representation – which enables her to cross boundaries and make links between the different disciplines of linguistics, literature, art and psychoanalysis. Like the semiotic, the abject forms part of Kristeva's own conceptual vocabulary and it is significant that since the early 1980s she has stopped using her own terminology and adopted the language of classical psychoanalysis, or terms belonging more generally to the literary and philosophical tradition.

I would like here to trace a link between the theory of abjection and Kristeva's work on melancholia. Whereas abjection corresponds to a structure evident in religion's definition of the sacred or a society's definition of taboo, melancholy corresponds to a clinical state as well as being a topos with its own cultural history. In *Soleil noir, dépression et mélancolie* (1983), Kristeva examines the link between depression and the history of melancholia in a literary, artistic and psychoanalytic context. Kristeva's work on depression is an integral part of her project to bring the unspeakable into desire and language. In depression there is a melancholic disinvestment in language's symbolic power, a split between language and affect. The melancholic communicates emotion or affect at the infra-verbal level of tone, modulation, vocal gesture, that is, a semiotic level. There is a failure of symbolic activity, a state of abjection, or a state Kristeva also refers to as *l'asymbolie*.

It is in her theory of melancholy that Kristeva is able to bring together aspects of the semiotic and of abjection. The clinical context for her own enquiry into melancholy is provided by the writings of Freud and Abraham and Torok as well as by her own clinical experience with patients.[11] Freud insisted on the distinction between mourning and melancholia, and Abraham and Torok, following Freud's model, re-define this distinction in terms of the difference between *introjection* and *incorporation*. Introjection is the metaphoric activity through which we acknowledge and symbolise loss; it characterises normal mourning. Melancholia or the failure of introjection takes the form of a fantasy of incorporation whereby the lost object is incorporated into the self in a fantasy guarding against its loss. The fantasy of incorporation is anti-metaphoric, taking literally that which only has figurative meaning. As Freud stresses, melancholia is the failure of the work of mourning.

Kristeva elaborates this model. So melancholia involves a paralysis of symbolic activity. The melancholic's energy is displaced from the social code. It is the energy of *déliaison* or unlinking: the deathdrive breaking symbolic links and meanings and shifting meaning therefore from the disinvested symbolic order to the semiotic realm of sounds, colours and rhythms, tone and modulation. In this it resembles the language of the poet. The language of the melancholic like the language of the poet is a primary representation of language and it is this fact and its therapeutic consequences that most interest Kristeva. In melancholia and poetic language there is a return to the very origins of language, to the poetic function as Jakobson understands it, a return from *signification* to *sens*. The listener or reader, deprived of obvious meaning, is faced with a secret language of hidden meanings over which the subject has imperious control, like the echolalia of the infant. The reader is left immersed in vocal gesture.

Illustration of Melancholy

It is no surprise then that Gérard de Nerval's sonnet 'El Desdichado', a fundamentally poetic and melancholic text, forms the focus of an analysis in *Soleil noir, dépression et mélancolie*.[12] Before demonstrating how Kristeva's theory of melancholy may lead us to a meaningful interpretation of this poem I would like to comment upon the specific character of Kristeva's treatment of the text. The very title of the essay 'Nerval, El Desdichado', in positing an equivalence between the poet and the subject of his poem, is a challenge to the anti-biographical polemic of structuralism and post-structuralism, the drive towards abstraction in which Kristeva herself participated. The title announces a significant return to the biographical subject and the commentary itself is a *tour de force* in boundary crossing between clinical, literary and poetic analysis, a disconcerting transgression of formal boundaries. I shall refer in more detail to the transgressive quality of much of Kristeva's writing later in this book.

What is interesting about 'Nerval, El Desdichado' is how it amalgamates clinical and poetic perspectives with great freedom, how it demonstrates the open structure of Julia Kristeva's attention to the symptoms presented by the melancholic subject of this poem and the attempt to recuperate this subject in an interpretation. Reading and analytic listening are very close here. In fact they are indissociable. I myself have analysed this poem's representation of melancholy in terms of vocal gesture and the transferential structures the text opens to the reader.[13] Kristeva's theory of melancholy as operating at an infraverbal level of communication is fundamental in my reading even if it does not form the focus of her own interpretation of this poem. Nerval's text is melancholic in the poetic sense of a return to the origins of language and in a concomitant clinical sense of a disinvestment in the symbolic capacity of language to function as a social code. The overdetermined naming in Nerval's poem does not function on the level of signification but calls out for a reading which attends to its pre-linguistic qualities and in this resembles music and painting rather than writing.

Kristeva has emphasised how the analyst must engage with the depressed patient on the pre-verbal level, must 'désarticuler la chaîne signifiante, en extraire le sens caché, par fragments, syllabes, groupe phonique'[14] (disarticulate the signifying chain, extract the hidden meaning, in fragments, syllables, phonic groups) and this is what is required of the reader of Nerval's text:

El Desdichado

Je suis le ténébreux, – le veuf, – l'inconsolé
Le prince d'Aquitaine à la tour abolie:
Ma seule *étoile* est morte, – et mon luth constellé
Porte le *Soleil* noir de la *Mélancolie*.

Dans la nuit du tombeau, toi qui m'as consolé,
Rends-moi le Pausilippe et la mer d'Italie,
la *fleur* qui plaisait tant à mon coeur désolé
Et la treille où le pampre à la rose s'allie.

Suis-je Amour ou Phébus? ... Lusignan ou Biron?
Mon front est rouge encor du baiser de la reine;
J'ai rêvé dans la grotte où nage la sirène ...

Et j'ai deux fois vainqueur traversé l'Achéron:
modulant tour à tour sur la lyre d'Orphée
Les soupirs de la sainte et les cris de la fée.

(Gérard de Nerval, *Les Filles de Feu*, 1854)

(I am the shadow, the widower, the unconsoled, the
Aquitanian prince with the ruined tower: my only *star*
is dead, and my star-strewn lute bears the *black sun of
Melancholy*. You who consoled me, in the night of the
tomb, give me back Posilipo and the Italian sea, the
flower which pleased my grief-stricken heart so much,
and the arbour where the vine joins with the rose.

Am I Love or Phoebus? ... Lusignan or Biron? My
brow is still red from the queen's kiss; I have dreamed
in the cave where the siren swims ... And I have twice
crossed Acheron victoriously: tuning in turn on
Orpheus's lyre the sighs of the saint and the fairy's
cries.)[15]

Reading Nerval's poem we might wonder how a text so
overdetermined on the level of mythical, magical reference
can sustain its affects, for, as so often with Nerval, we are
bewildered by a myriad of mythical, cultural, geographical
proper nouns but held undeterred by the aesthetic and

emotive qualities of the writing. In this poem the meaning of the language must be seen to have shifted from a disinvested symbolic order to the semiotic realm of sounds, colours and rhythms – like the language of the melancholic. If one reads the text aloud there can be no denying the vocalic force of the poem, the primacy of voice and of song. There is of course semantic interference into the prosody but a vocalic reading gives a sense of pattern and repetition and connectedness which the poem lacks on the semantic level. The music derived from the repetition of the vowel-sounds *o é i a* and *y* and diphthongs *ui oi u* and *an* comes as if from a musical score made up of the notes *la mi re sol*, the mute *e*, the extraneous *y* as if from 'luth', and the diphthongs as chords. Assonantal patterns produce echoes and create phonic groups, which constantly intersect, repeat and echo each other. This is language decomposed to its syllabic origins, to *poesis*, to vocalics and their patterning into musicality. It is a primary representation of language in which rhythm and sound are privileged over semantic meaning. The 'mysticisme de la souffrance', mystic quality of suffering, which Kristeva finds represented semiotically in the language of the melancholic is here represented prosodically in the poem. The title, which functions on many levels, also functions vocalically: El Desdichado.

If 'El Desdichado' is one deprived of language, or one who, like the melancholic, is a stranger to his own language, then it is a certain kind of reading, attentive to semiotic modalities, that can restore language to its origin. In her analysis of melancholico-depressive symptoms, Kristeva sees the transferential relationship, which is the fundamental structure of analysis, as an ideal therapeutic space for treating the melancholic patient and their suspension of the social code. Her reading of the representation of sensation in a space between *sens* and *signification* in the language of Proust is an analogical model of this space for interpretation. Attention to the representation of sensation and of drives involves, she argues, as analyst or reader, entering into a heterogeneous psychic space. This is the space into which Nerval's poem invites the reader since the melancholic text places the reader outside the social code, in the realm of the lost object and of displaced desire.

Female Melancholy

It has often been been remarked that the publication of *Histoires d'amour* in 1983 and *Pouvoirs de l'horreur* in 1987 marked a change in Kristeva's style and the emergence of a new kind of subjectivity. In *Histoires d'amour* Kristeva moves from the academic 'nous' to return to her text in the first person singular; the first line reads,

> Aussi loin que je me rappelle mes amours, je trouve difficile d'en parler.

> (From as far back as I remember my lovelife, I find it difficult to talk about it.)

Then in 1987 the first line of *Sn* announces both the I and the reader, 'J'essaie de vous parler d'un gouffre de tristesse' (I am going to try to talk to you about a gulf of sadness). This change cannot be divorced from Kristeva's involvement in psychoanalysis, that is, both personal analysis and practice as an analyst. It is furthermore an aspect of Kristeva's work which has become increasingly apparent, the emergence of a freer style in which both disconcertingly and engagingly Julia Kristeva represents her subjectivity and her intellectual biography to her readers. This amalgamation of subjectivity and traditional philosophical writing frequently disconcerts the French establishment, as it disconcerts individual readers in different ways. The psychoanalytic establishment might argue for a more distinctly clinical approach, the literary establishment for a clearer demarcation of one's discipline.

These critical responses are as symptomatic of problems of subjective and collective identity as they are symptomatic of Kristeva's need to find a form of expression which integrates fantasy and philosophy, personal history and social history, literary analysis and clinical observation. The reader, unsure of the status of the text, is compelled either to react against such startling heterogeneity or to engage with the text on a different level in a structure of non-hierarchy tantamount to psychoanalytic listening.

Representing and giving meaning to the primarily unsayable is at the heart of Kristeva's project and the pre-oedipal archaic relation of the girl-infant with the mother belongs to this ineffable realm. From *Sn*, in which she devotes a chapter to the specificity of female depression, Kristeva commits herself to opening up and verbalising this hermetic layer of female sexuality.[16] Her study in *Sn* refers to three figures of female depression whose symptoms might be roughly defined as 'le corps-tombeau' – the body as a crypt; 'la perversion blanche' – a form of perversion manifest in blind devotion to duty, and 'la vierge mère' – virginal motherhood. Each figure represents an addiction to what Kristeva calls 'la chose maternelle' – the maternal thing, that is, a melancholic non-separation from the figure of the mother.

I would like to comment on a literary representation of female melancholia which provides a perfect illustration of Kristeva's figures of female depression. Balzac's *Eugénie Grandet* tells the story of a mother and her daughter locked in a fusional melancholic relationship.[17] Eugénie Grandet and her mother have spent every day for the last fifteen years sitting together in the womb-like Grandet living-room maintaining the household linen. Not only the living-room but the whole of monsieur Grandet's house represents the mother–daughter relationship. They sleep separated only by a glass door; and these bizarre sleeping arrangements along with the description of the room where they spend their lives, and a later image of their being attached to each other like Siamese twins, are all symptomatic of fusion, identification and incestuous claustrophobia. This state of pre-oedipal fusion is as oppressive as the law of the father represented by the terrifying figure of *le père Grandet* for, if we follow Kristeva's theory, it is equally totalitarian. It is related to what she calls the paralysis of the abject position, between the infancy of the pre-oedipal and access to language in the symbolic. The internalisation of lost objects prevalent in melancholy is a similar boundary state, and it is the state of melancholy which I should like to examine further here in so far as it is a defining structure in Balzac's text.

The structuring principle of Eugénie Grandet's world is female melancholy, in which mother and daughter are bound together in a state of mournful non-differentiation. In this sense, the failure of symbolic or metaphoric activity which Kristeva associates with melancholy and the concomitant fantasy of incorporation defined above in relation to Abraham and Torok, are evident in a close reading of *Eugénie Grandet*. They are readable in the pseudo-realist description of the house at Saumur and its evocation of degradation and depoetisation. Eugénie Grandet is trapped in a world of impossible fusion with a mother whose reaction to any perturbation is to 'faire la mort' or play dead. Dutybound to Grandet, she and her daughter live in the space delimited by his moods and after her mother's death Eugénie will virtually live the life of a mystic bound to her mother's dying words. Their life corresponds closely to the three figures of female depression defined by Kristeva in *Soleil noir*, the female body as a crypt for the lost object; perverse devotion to duty, destiny, fatality; and self-enclosure in a pre-symbolic space against the threats of the outside world. Kristeva, like Freud and Abraham and Torok, sees a certain form of metaphoric activity as melancholy's ultimate prevention and cure and Eugénie Grandet has an opening for metaphoric activity – in romance – when she falls in love with her cousin

Charles. When this moment arrives for Eugénie she interests herself in her appearance for the first time in her life, wakes early and dresses with care. As she looks out of her window awaiting her cousin she watches the garden which, despite being bathed in the sunlight of her new love, hosts a sinister scenario. The plants are tangled, withered and blighted, the walls are covered in dank rotting plants and the steps leading to the garden gate are compared to the tomb of a knight buried by his widow during the religious crusades, an image of encrypting proper to Eugénie Grandet's melancholy, Kristeva's first figure of female melancholy. In falling in love with Charles she falls in love with an image of melancholy, and long after he has disappeared from the scene she nurses his image for nine years waiting for his return. Her sexual awakening and the glimmers of hope which enter the narrative with it, such as sunlight on the blighted garden, is coded by this central image of mourning and by references to a melancholic lack of self-regard against the terror of her father. For at the very moment that Eugénie Grandet might break out of that fusional relationship with her mother she is literally terrorised by the figure of an all-powerful father. This is because the mother's position in the oedipal triangle is masked by implacable devotion to duty, destiny, fatality. Eugénie Grandet's mother leaves her daughter no access to symbolic activity. She dies from identifying literally with her daughter who is beaten by her father and leaves her with the dying words that there is only happiness in heaven ... After her father's death, with now the priest as master of her fate, Eugénie Grandet is proposed two possible paths: marriage or voluntary celibacy. She chooses a death in life, proper to her melancholy. She chooses to marry and remain celibate. This corresponds to Kristeva's third figure of female melancholy which is described as 'entering into motherhood as if one were entering a convent'.[18] Here the character enters into marriage as if she were entering a convent. In this novel Balzac links the bourgeois tragedy to a certain structure of femininity, a melancholic structure, which is closely related to the mother–daughter relationship. The novel provides a perfect illustration of this aspect of female melancholia whereby the subject closes in on herself, self-protectively, against entering into culture.

So the retreat into the enclosure of melancholy is closely related to Kristeva's definition of the abject and is characteristic of the enclosure of the mother–daughter relationship. The French philosopher and feminist Luce Irigaray refers to such female melancholia as a state of 'dereliction' and argues that the masculinist bias of Western metaphysics traps femininity in an unrepresentable, melancholic position and women as objects of exchange in the male imaginary. According to Irigaray women remain trapped in this position because there does not exist a language which adequately represents and mediates the mother–daughter relationship. The girl-child has no representation of what has been lost.[19] Kristeva might argue that whereas male artists and writers might celebrate the mother-figure or the love of the mother as something they have partly relinquished, this is a much more complex issue for the woman, whose survival depends on the kind of balancing act I describe in Chapter 4.

The question of female melancholia and its relation to the maternal might be seen to find an answer in *Histoires d'amour* (1983), the answer which precedes the question of *Soleil noir* (1987).

CHAPTER 3

Transference, Time, Literary Experience

Transference

Histoires d'amour, which Kristeva published in 1983, might be read in close relation to *Soleil noir, dépression et mélancolie*, which she published in 1987; stories of love, stories of sadness, each providing the lining for the other and evolving in close correlation.

While presenting a history of love in Western culture, *Histoires d'amour* is primarily about the therapeutic value of transference love, that is, the imitation of love which takes place in the analytic cure,

> C'est parce que nous manquons aujourd'hui de propre, couverts de tant d'abjections, et que les jalons qui assuraient l'ascension vers le bien se sont avérés douteux, que nous avons des crises d'amour ... L'expérience amoureuse noue indissolublement le symbolique (ce qui est interdit, discernable, pensable), l'imaginaire (ce que le Moi se représente pour se soutenir et s'agrandir) et le réel (cet impossible où les affects aspirent à tout et il n'y a personne pour tenir compte du fait que je ne suis qu'une partie).[1]

> It is because we suffer today from a lack of what is proper to us, covered as we are by so many abjections, and because the signposts which guaranteed our ascension towards the good have turned out to be dubious, that we suffer from crises of love ... The experience of love ties together indissolubly the symbolic (that which is

forbidden, discernable, thinkable), the imaginary (what
the Ego imagines to support itself and grow) and the
real (the realm of the impossible where the emotions
aspire to everything and where there is nobody to take
account of the fact that I am only a part of the whole).

Premier des modernes, un postromantique, Sigmund
Freud s'avise de faire de l'amour une cure.[2]

A post-romantic and first among modern thinkers,
Sigmund Freud takes it upon himself to make a cure
out of love.

In Kristeva's thinking, both writing and art, the maternal
ethic – the mother's socialisation of the infant through
language – and psychoanalysis, all have an important,
transitional status in that they inscribe the realm of the
imaginary within a socio-cultural, symbolic process. The
openness to the imagination inherent in writing, art and
love enables the naming and symbolisation of that which
remains unspeakable in the established vernacular, and thus
breaks the silences and taboos which structure the social
hierarchy. For the writer, or the patient in analysis, or the
growing child, such an activity involves a constant renegotiation of the frontiers and structures which organise
and constrain his imagination. He is rather like a stage-
director faced with adapting his inspiration to a limited
budget. It is a labour of love. Transitional activities are
hard work since the imaginary must be made constantly
aware of the demands of the symbolic, and as the individual
grows in subjectivity he is bound to play with the rules and
at times revolt against them and transgress. This revolt is
both disgust at the reminder of what is now forbidden by
the laws and taboos which structure the socialised
individual, and a reaction in the name of subjectivity at
the suppression exerted by those laws. The lining of that
revolt is the boundary state of abjection. Yet art and
psychoanalysis enable the representation and verbalisation

of those sensations and symptoms which have remained unspeakably close to the body since ordinary language has neither contained or expressed them. This happens transgressively, in writing, in literary language which infringes the laws of fixed syntax and grammar, and in analysis through the transference.

Just as the mother should provide a bridge for the child's difficult passage into language, the analyst provides a bridge for the patient's verbalisation of repressed material. The analyst is an agent of connections who, like the mother, is inscribed in an ethic of love, loving the patient/child, while situating their own desire outside that relationship. In analysis the ethic of love demands a knowledge of transference. Transference is an unconscious process whereby the patient transfers onto the figure of the analyst the unresolved demands, conflicts and emotions of his personal history. It is hardly surprising that, in analysis, given the background of unresolved emotional demand, transference imitates falling in love, love in the sense of the Greek *eros*, violent, painful love, and the Christian *agape*, love tending towards the Platonic ideal. Kristeva's particular contribution to a theory of the transference lies in her emphasis on identification, the analyst's identification with the patient's symptoms through a shared language which speaks the body. We have seen that in her work on depression Kristeva draws attention to a melancholic disinvestment in language's symbolic power whereby the melancholic communicates emotion or affect at the infra-verbal level of tone, modulation or vocal gesture. Treating depression then involves the analyst's recognition of and identification with this pre-verbal realm of expression. The analyst participates in the transference, while providing a framework for its expression. Abject subjectivity can then cross the boundary from the enclosure of a pre-oedipal, fusional relationship with the mother's body, which we saw in Chapter 2, to the relative

tranquillity and distance of an idealising kind of love, for
the father, in the symbolic.

   Kristeva's description of this move from primary identification or narcissism to idealisation in the first chapter
of *Histoires d'amour* makes abundantly clear her
commitment to the therapeutic value of such a process:

> le génie de Freud ... il dissocie en fait l'idéalisation (et
> avec elle la relation amoureuse) du corps à corps entre
> mère et enfant, et introduit le Tiers comme condition
> de la vie psychique en tant qu'elle est une vie
> amoureuse.[3]

> The genius of Freud lies in his dissociation of idealisation
> (and of the relationship of love) from the fusional
> mother–child relationship and his introduction of the
> third party as a condition of the life of the psyche in so
> far as that in itself is a condition of love.

I do not think Kristeva's emphasis here amounts to an
idealisation of father-figures but rather to an insistence upon
the symbolic function of idealisation, what Lacan calls the
symbolic importance of the phallus, as the sign of a salutary
exit from fusion with the mother-figure. The analyst too
must occupy this oedipal position of third party, must play
across all registers. While claiming that analysts have
often neglected or ignored archaic, pre-oedipal material
associated with the mother, Kristeva argues both that this
area must be addressed and that today's therapists are often
required to assume a paternal, symbolic function, to
reinstate the law of the father. Once the patient recognises
her desire in relation to these two poles, maternal and
paternal, she has recognised the nostalgia for maternal
fusion, the disturbance caused by seduction, the law
against incest, and is finally free to construct (this) reality
as a more or less fragile border of her lovelife.

   This analysis of love in *Histoires d'amour* is a measure
of Kristeva's commitment to a language which nurtures

psychic health, that is both freedom and security. It is the background to an ethics of identity some consider conservative. It is the background to her resistance to espouse a feminist politics which involves separatism. Furthermore it encapsulates that conviction in the creative potential of transgression within movable boundaries which has always characterised her thought just as it encapsulates her own ability to be at once a transgressive and a committed public thinker. Some reactions to what is construed as Kristeva's conservatism were discussed in Chapter 2. The debate Kristeva provokes among American feminists such as Stone, Oliver and Jardine cannot be dissociated from the issues of translation, exile and cultural difference which I outlined in my introduction and which are being addressed throughout this book. Kristeva will continue to disconcert Anglo-American feminists and masculinists alike, while seducing their European counterparts.

So Kristeva elaborates a theory of sexual identity which involves an evolution from primary identification or narcissism to a sublimatory idealisation of the father-figure in the form of a certain acceptance of the law, that is, the law of sexual difference, of generational difference and the law against incest. This evolution takes place in the transference. In literature the writing of Joyce embodies the transferential process of identification for it reveals the writer's capacity to cross the boundaries of sexual and generational identity and to represent pre-verbal experience poetically, through the use of the semiotic in a symbolic creation. Yet Kristeva's emphasis on Joyce's use of the semiotic differs from *Tel Quel*'s love-affair with Joycean textuality, which, in distinguishing writing from speech, overlooked orality – that is, the inscription of the pre-verbal in writing. For Kristeva, pre-verbal experience takes the form of colour, sound and gesture, which enter the text as a transgression of the coded boundaries of syntax, grammar and sexual identity. She remarks upon the

extraordinary plasticity of Joyce's writing, the malleability
and multiplicity which is characteristic of his polymorphous
subjectivity and polyphonic text. A link is sketched in *Les
nouvelles maladies de l'âme (Lnma)* between Joyce's iden-
tificatory powers with his characters, identifications which
are both corporeal and metaphysical, and the analyst's
involvement in the transference, or counter-transference,
that is, the analyst's recognition of her own desire. The
counter-transference, argues Kristeva, can be used as an
instrument which operates at once on the hysterical level
of bodily identification and on the subliminal and creative
level of participating in a cure or text which brings
symptoms and ineffabilities into speech.

Time

In an interview, published in *L'Infini* in 1994 about her
book *Les nouvelles maladies de l'âme*, Kristeva describes this
link between Joyce's writing and analytic activity:

> L'expérience de Joyce est pour moi une expérience trans-
> théologique de l'écriture. Son oeuvre entretient une
> connivence avec les thèmes de l'incarnation et de la
> transsubstantiation. Il met en acte l'idée que le Verbe
> peut se faire chair, que l'écriture peut nous réincarner.
> Cette utilisation particulière du langage suppose une
> capacité identificatoire avec l'autre, avec le monde,
> les sons, les odeurs, ainsi qu'avec l'autre sexe, comme
> on le voit quand le narrateur s'incarne dans des
> personnages féminins. Cette plasticité, présente au
> coeur de l'alchimie du langage de Joyce, lui permet de
> passer de l'idée à l'être. L'écrivain est dans l'être, pas
> dans le signifiant seul. A mon sens, cette expérience
> représente un modèle pour l'analyste.[4]

> Experience in Joyce is for me a trans-theological
> experience of writing. His work maintains a connivance
> with the themes of incarnation and of transubstanti-

ation. It practises the idea that the word can be made flesh, that writing can be a reincarnation. This particular use of language assumes a capacity for identification with the other, with the world, with sounds and smells, as well as with the opposite sex, as we see when the narrator becomes embodied in female characters. That plasticity which is present at the heart of the alchemy of Joyce's language allows him to move from the idea to Being. The writer is in Being, not isolated in the signifier. For me, that experience represents a model for the analyst.

Les nouvelles maladies de l'âme is very much a book in which Kristeva can be seen as a clinician treating symptoms of malaise in contemporary culture. The reference to soul in the title might appear religious or metaphysical but Kristeva insists that soul here is to be understood as a heterogeneous construction, between the physical and the metaphysical, which draws upon Freud's dualist conception of the psyche as doubly determined by the laws of biology and those of language. Thinking about the soul in this way enables the analyst to wait at the crossroads between the symbolic and the somatic, or between language and the body. It enables the reader of literature or the cultural historian to be at once attentive to economies of desire or sexuality as well as to literary, religious or cultural sublimations of this energy which enable subjectivity to be inscribed in mankind and individuals to participate in Being.

In *Lnma* Kristeva is concerned with a breakdown in fundamental imaginative activities such as reading, personal creativity, self-expression and representing one's emotions. It is this breakdown which modern man proclaims in psycho-somatic symptoms, symptoms of exhaustion, depression and manic behaviour which he alleviates provisionally with pills or immersion in today's spectator society. The new maladies of the soul are the symptoms

of this breakdown of the Imaginary to which Kristeva
draws our attention and which can be attributed to the
surfeit of non-verbal, non-verbalised images which
characterise today's spectator society:

> Notre société produit sans doute beaucoup d'images,
> mais tant que leur sens nous reste étranger elles ne
> nourrissent pas notre vie imaginaire.[5]

> There is no doubt that our society produces many
> images, but while their meaning remains estranged
> from us they cannot enter our Imaginary.

In a world dominated by the screen, the small screen, the
big screen, the cyberspace, there is no time and space for
the slow processing of the dark-room. We are all submitted
to the facile absorption of images and information but those
images bear no relation to the subjective work of the
imagination, and that information does not bear the mark
of experience. In the virtual time and space of global
networks and information systems there are few limits, there
is no time and space for subjectivity to define itself, that
is, to seek expression, encounter obstacles, imagine ways
round them, to resign itself to the inevitable and revolt
against the impossible. Psychoanalysis and literature are
the guardians of the time and space of subjective experience
and the writers who both provide us with and demand of
us a time and space accorded to the exploration of
subjectivity and of sexual desire, and their encounter with
society, their place in culture, are Joyce, and Proust, the
subject of Kristeva's *Le temps sensible*. Theirs is the time
and space of a revolt which is fundamentally poetic.

The notion of time is important in *Lnma* which, in
clinical and literary analyses, attempts to restore time in
a cyclical non-linear sense which nevertheless inserts itself
into history. This sort of time is the time of the analytic
cure, transforming the linear logic of money into the
circular logic of time as evolution. Kristeva's formulation

is that psychoanalysis transforms money into time. Analysis and literature provide a respite from the treadmill demands of linear time and in so doing they are reparative. In the analytic encounter then the transference relationship will embody and permit the elaboration of a time of remembrance. It will interrupt the smooth flow of linear time. It will be time-consuming. But it will provide a space for the representation of those dissociations and splittings – repressed memories and the defences they generate – which punctuate the life of the individual in a painful and repeated way. Kristeva explains how the analyst's participation in the transference can, for example, repair the temporal dissociations apparent in the suffering of the hysteric.

In hysteria there is a dissociation between communication, identity, social skills in present time, and symptoms such as fits and paralysis which screen repressed memories and reveal emotion and excitability which cannot be properly verbalised. The analyst's insight and controlled identification with the patient's symptoms, in stimulating associations between symptom and memory, can help repair the dissociations and bring the patient to a fuller, more integrated temporality,

> Pouvoir écouter l'hystérique en se présentant comme un miroir possible permet une compréhension très fine de son discours dans son rapport au corps et à la pulsion. Cela dit, le retrait de l'analyste est nécessaire également pour permettre au patient de trouver la traduction psychique de la pulsion qu'il a été amené à reconnaître.[6]

The capacity to listen to the hysteric while presenting oneself as a possible mirror permits a very fine comprehension of their discourse in relation to the body and to the drives. That said, it is just as necessary for the analyst to withdraw, to permit the patient to find her own psychical translation or verbal formulation of the drive, the excitability, which has been brought to recognition.

C'est à l'écoute de l'hystérie que Freud a élaboré la pierre angulaire de sa théorie, à savoir le modèle de l'inconscient. La cure des hystériques constitue l'origine de la psychanalyse.[7]

It was while listening to hysteria that Freud elaborated the cornerstone of his theory, that is, the model of the unconscious. The cure of the hysterics constitutes the origin of psychoanalysis.

In the same way, in the essay 'L'enfant au sens indicible', 'the child with inexpressible meaning', a chapter of *Lnma* which recounts the case of a depressed child who was unable to speak, Kristeva demonstrates how by identifying with the child's pre-verbal retreat into a space outside language, by singing with the child, she was able to elaborate a transitional space of communication, a space incorporating both the grammatical categories of the symbolic and the heterogeneity of the semiotic. For Kristeva, discourse is a complex psychical phenomenon which cannot be reduced to the arrangement of grammatical categories – to the symbolic, for language is heterogeneous and necessarily includes semiotic modalities:

En elle se déploient les représentants psychiques des affects et, avec eux, la dramaturgie des loisirs, des peurs et des dépressions qui ont un sens pour l'enfant même s'il ne parvient pas à s'inscrire dans la signification codée de la langue d'usage.[8]

All the psychical representatives of affect are deployed (in language) and with them the dramaturgy of desires, fears, depressions which have a meaning for the child even if he is not capable of submitting to the coded signification of a common language.

What *Lnma* introduces, and what *Lts* and *Snsr* perpetuate, is that exploration of a transitional time and space embodied in literature and in analysis and which is occupied by a type of dreamwork. In a lecture at a conference on literature and dream held at the Institut Charlemagne in 1996, Kristeva made clear her commitment as literary critic and clinician and indeed as a writer of fiction, to the creation of forms of expression and representation for our unspeakable thoughts. Speaking the unspeakable, representing the unrepresentable are the premises of the work of psychoanalysis, of interpreting texts and of writing poetic fiction. In order for this to take place the work of the unconscious and of imaginary processes needs to be symbolised. The account of the dream is a perfect model of this process. The unrepresentable may find representation in a type of dreamwork which makes visible and, in the account of the dream, brings into language images and emotion which otherwise have no access to the visible or to language. What then is the relationship between the unrepresentable and meaning in literature? In order to express things we find difficult to name literature has to reinvent language, to reveal hidden territories introducing the exorbitant and the unknown. It is the function of dream and the preoccupation of literature to be as close as possible to the unnameable.

Literary Experience

Kristeva's novel *Le viel homme et les loups* was written to symbolise and verbalise an ineffable loss, the loss of her father as a result of a medical experiment in an East European hospital. It is a work of mourning in the form of a fiction which imagines death and the dreams of the dying man. Words and sensation occupy that transitional space between unrepresentable suffering and symbolisation. The image, that of Goya's painting, also has a place in this space leading to verbalisation. In *Lts*, her work on Proust, Kristeva relates this transitional space to her analysis of what she calls the dream of the second apartment. In the 1970s Kristeva elaborated the idea of a sensory cavern, which she called the *chora*, to describe a pre-verbal space inhabited by sensation, which is inaccessible to the mind and outside time. Let us relate this to desire and to the need to communicate, and say that in Proust there is a dissociation between the two, a *décalage* which will be filled and represented by the style of *A la recherche*. In this sense we can say that the writer succeeds in inhabiting that gap which separates autism from the world of communication. The writer finds words, images, and evokes sensations. He creates a style which at both a figurative and verbal level represents the unrepresentable, says the ineffable. In analysis the presence and words of the analyst provide that transitional bridge between the unrepresentable energy and emotion of archaic, unconscious reality and either figurative or verbal symbolisation. So Kristeva introduces a supplementary third dimension into the Lacanian model of the imaginary and the symbolic, a transitional sensory space we can call the semiotic and which is occupied by sensation, vocalics and images. It is a pre-oedipal, narcissistic domain between the non-differentiation of the imaginary and the set structures of the symbolic. This is the space of the *camera obscura*, a dark-room or processing room outside time and removed from the demands of the social code. It is a maternal space from which the figure of the father is not absent, but rather prefigured.

In a recent interview in *L'Infini* Kristeva reiterates her insistence upon the importance of the maternal. She considers that recent psychoanalytic thought, especially Lacanian psychoanalysis, has not paid sufficient attention to the maternal. According to Kristeva it is as important to draw attention to the fundamental place of the mother, that is, the place of archaic imagos of the mother which occupy our imaginary, as it is to put her in her place in the socio-cultural space – in the symbolic. Once we can understand the role played in our fantasy life by the archaic mother figure we can achieve some distance from the power she holds in that realm. We can put her in her proper place:

> Je profiterai ici de votre question pour souligner l'importance du lieu maternel auquel je pense que les courants psychanalytiques récents, Lacaniens notamment, n'ont pas suffisamment rendu hommage. La fonction maternelle, selon moi, doit être habilitée, comme la nécessité de prendre ses distances vis-à-vis d'elle. C'est d'ailleurs à la femme qu'il revient de favoriser cette mise à distance de celui qui est une partie d'elle-même: l'enfant. On mesure là l'immense rôle culturel des mères – un rôle dans lequel on n'est donc pas étonné de les voir assez souvent échouer.[9]

> I shall take advantage of your question to emphasise the importance of the maternal to which I consider recent psychoanalytic thought, especially Lacanian psychoanalysis, has not paid sufficient homage. It is my opinion that the maternal function must be rehabilitated as must the necessity of taking one's distance from it. Besides it comes down to the woman to foster that process of distancing between herself and the one who is a part of herself: the child. This is a measure of the immense cultural role of mothers – a role in which it is hardly surprising to see that they fail often enough.

By reintroducing the vital importance of the maternal into analytic thought Kristeva, in *Lnma*, adds her own dimension to the seminal cases of psychoanalytic literature. These concern Freud's treatment of hysteria and obsessional neurosis in the form of the cases of 'Dora' and 'The Ratman'. What Freud failed to address in the Dora case, says Kristeva, is the question of maternal fixation, of the pre-oedipal, archaic mother–daughter relationship and so the question of latent female homosexuality or what Kristeva calls primary homosexuality. I shall return to this question in more detail in Chapter 4. What he failed to address in the case of the Ratman is the oral nature of the Ratman's fantasies, which leads him to eliminate the question of orality, the question of the archaic mother–infant relationship, in his analysis of this case. Kristeva does not fail to associate this omission to an evident problematic relation to orality in Freud's own history. It is in his study of female sexuality that Freud recognises that the archaic mother–daughter relationship, like the Minoan-Mycenaean civilisation beneath the civilisation of Greece, is a hidden layer of femininity and is of particularly difficult access because subject to powerful repression.[10] According to Kristeva, and I think this is an important current in modern psychoanalytic thought on female sexuality, which women analysts have explored and male analysts neglected, this archaic relation is the source of an endogenous homosexuality which is constitutive of femininity in general.

Freud was fond of archeological metaphors which enabled him to describe the psyche as an intricate composition of stratae. To distinguish the atemporality of the history of the psyche from man's evolution through history, he talks about ontogenesis as opposed to phylogenesis. Lacan, referring to the psyche's linguistic history, makes a similar distinction between *lalangue* and *parlêtre*. With the terms ontogenesis and *lalangue* both thinkers are formulating the existence of the infantile, Freud, in terms of the biology of the individual as opposed to the evolution of the race and Lacan, in terms of the pre-verbal language of the infant as opposed to social discourse. They associate their formulation of the infantile with the maternal continent but it is Kristeva who dares to plunge into the heart of the unsayable and to try to bring it into language.

Bringing the unsayable into language is no easy task, neither for the writer nor the analyst, and transitional forms of symbolisation mark the path to verbalisation. In this sense the image is transitional and may be used as such in the psychoanalytic cure, as Kristeva shows in the essay 'L'âme et l'image' in *Lnma,* which presents the case-study of a patient whose pictures formed part of the analytic material. In this sense the image is transitional between unconscious material and language in the symbolic, as indeed is the imaginary. But links must be formulated between the image, language and the unconscious if modern man is to survive the big screen and spectator society. So the image, in Kristeva, is ambivalent and I suspect Kristeva has more to say about this ambivalence in future work.

A picture is emerging, which, announced in *Pdh* and moving through *Hd'a* and *Sn* to *Lnma,* represents Kristeva's personal contribution as a woman intellectual, mother and analyst to analytic thought. This is a fundamental emphasis on the archaic mother, the imagined mother, which, supplementing Lacanian preoccupation with the sign and Freudian preoccupation with the drives, marks out the work on melancholia, hysteria, sensory experience and its relation to verbalisation. Furthermore this concentration on the relationship between the body and language introduces Kristeva's more recent concern with the notions of literary experience and transubstantiation, which, examining the writer's participation in Being, or *l'Etre,* provides the philosophical framework for *Lts* and is moreover an important link in the theory of revolt. The theory of revolt encompasses the whole trajectory, since it explores the etymological evolution of the term revolt and leads back to *la révolution* of *La révolution du langage poétique.* It also contains the notion of revolt as horror or a visceral reaction against boundaries or limits announced in *Pdh.* Furthermore it leads to the elaboration of the Freudian and Proustian sense of the term revolt in *Lts,* and finally to the enquiry into the limits and possibilities of revolt in psychical and literary experience which is presented in *Snsr.*

The text which introduces the theory of revolt and
provides a link between *Lts* and earlier and later work,
appeared in *L'Infini* in the winter of 1994. It is a short
conference paper named 'Monstrueuse intimité',
'Monstrous Intimacy', and subtitled 'Literature as
Experience', which was given at the Nobel symposium
'Language and Mind' in Stockholm, August 1994. In
this text Kristeva begins by elaborating the etymology
of revolt,

> ... un retour, une reprise du passé en vue d'un
> déplacement, d'une interrogation, un sarcasme,
> contestation, insolence, rupture.[11]

> ... a return, a re-engagement with the past envisaging
> a displacement, an interrogation, a derision, a
> contestation, an impertinence, a break with the past.

The difference between the text and its translation is
symptomatic. English cannot reproduce the Proustian
resonances of the French prefix *re* – 'à la recherche', 'le
temps retrouvé' – the notion of repeated action, of looking
and finding again and again, of experiencing. Nor can it
evoke the psychoanalytic resonances of such an enterprise
and its linking to the etymology of *revolvere*, of revolution
and therefore *révolte* as going back, returning, turning
inside out and remembering, as anamnesis. We need to
be within a Romance etymology to understand the full
import of Kristeva's Proustian and Freudian elaboration
of the term *revolvere*. She relies upon the play of literary
and philosophical echoes contained within the word and
its etymology, and this enquiry will in fact form part of
the first chapter of *Snsr*.[12]

In 'Monstrous Intimacy' Kristeva is the first to put her
theory of *révolte* into practice, for in this piece theorising
revolutionary displacement she opens with an interrogation
of structuralism's preoccupation with the sign and cites
three thinkers who might be seen to have embodied this,

'Jakobson, Barthes, Kristeva'. So the piece begins with a return, an interrogation of past practice and a suggestion that we might now make a displacement from this to the notion of literature as experience. This is no refutation of earlier work, or of the thinking of predecessors. It is Kristeva in practice constantly interrogating fixed identities and establishing herself as a subject in process, evolving through different boundaries in time. The word experience is here used as a philosophical term encompassing thought, emotional life, the sensible, sexuality and fantasy-life. The word is being used in a particular philosophical sense, both Hegelian and Heideggerean, to refer to the subject's participation in Being. This might be construed as fusion with the presence of God and therefore as religious experience, or as the subject's identification with man, with what Merleau-Ponty calls the flesh of the world, 'la chair du monde', a phenomenological experience. Kristeva's theory is that both literary and analytic discourse, through the process of identification, link subjectivity to a sphere outside immediate subjectivity. This realm beyond subjectivity is a sort of collective unconscious which is both spiritual and corporeal, and the process through which language participates in lived experience she compares to transubstantiation, the word made flesh, the subject's participation in Being. Transubstantiation is a term from Catholic theology which evokes man's communion with the divine in the Eucharist – which literally and metaphorically involves an incorporation. It is a sacrament, a place for forgiveness and for grace, 'un lieu de pardon et de grâce', a gift of meaning and transcendence.

How can writing be experienced as an inscription of the body we might ask? How can it represent the senses in a way that erases the borders of individuals and their bodies and be experienced as *jouissance*, that is, unspeakable sensual pleasure? Kristeva takes Proust's use of metaphor and Joyce's use of identification to argue what she has always argued, that the transgressions of literary language are a poetic inscription of that which is beyond language, the body, the drives, the unrepresentable, unspeakable. This was the thesis of *La révolution du langage poétique* (1974) and it is not difficult to see that *révolution* here can be reread retrospectively within the etymology of *revolvere* as interrogation, displacement, remembrance.

The notion of time, 'le temps', is fundamental. Revolt and revolution in the Freudian, Proustian sense must integrate time, and time must integrate the fixed entities of cursive history as much as it does the fluid entities of monumental personal history. The Proustian time of involuntary memory links present and past sensation metaphorically. It is a time of remembrance and association, a fundamentally analytic psychical time. When the narrator of *A la recherche du temps perdu* (1909) remembers how as an adult tasting a madeleine dipped in tea he was transported back on a wave of perfumed sensation – taste and smell – to a moment of his childhood long forgotten, he is bringing together three moments in time: writing, remembering and primary experience.

In his essay 'Creative Writers and Daydreaming' (1908), Freud relates creative writing, daydreaming, fantasy, to three times, three tenses, linked by the desire which traverses them: an intense experience in the present awakens a past experience, usually belonging to childhood.[13] The amalgam of these two moments produces the desire to imagine, represent, give expression to the moment of remembrance. This third time or tense, which for Freud is 'the time of the literary work' is what Proust calls 'le temps retrouvé'/time rediscovered and Kristeva 'l'expérience du temps incorporé'/the experience of incorporated time or 'le temps sensible'/sentient time.

It would be helpful here to consider Kristeva's theory of *le temps sensible* as it appears in her book on Proust. Time in Proust is an association of two sensations. Past sensation inhabits us. Involuntary memory returns to it when a present perception associated with the past, as Freud argues, by the desire which traverses time, links up with the past. Sensations are linked to the body and an association is a metaphor. Proust's metaphors are lined with sensation. They are not metaphors in the way formalist rhetoric understands metaphor: the replacement of a hackneyed or abstract term by an unusual, displaced term. They are analogies – maintaining two different terms in reciprocity or contradiction. We cannot talk about the word or the sign as the minimal element of Proust's writing. We have to talk about an amalgam of the sensation and the idea, of the image incarnate. When sensations are associated in this way across time and space, they lose their specificity and become impression. This impression can be shared with the reader as a sensory experience. Proustian time inscribes the body in language. Thus sensation teaches us the living relationship between the perceiving subject, his body and his world. The reader's participation in the sensory experience is a communion, an identification with something both at once inside and outside himself. This real and symbolic presence in sensation recalls the complexity of sacrament in theological discourse and Merleau-Ponty's account of 'le sensible' in phenomenology. So sentient time, *le temps sensible*, integrating the movement of history and personal history is what enables images and text to emerge from the silences of the dark-room. Sentient time is characteristic of certain forms of writing as it is characteristic of the analytic cure.

Revolution and Revolt

I would like now to turn to discuss the transgressive nature of Kristeva's writing and boundary crossing since thoughts about transgression have characterised readings of the texts cited above and the question casts interesting light upon Kristeva's work as a whole.

In *Lts*, Kristeva juxtaposes literary analysis with references to patients' case-histories and personal reflections. This has been seen as a transgressive activity which destabilises our idea of discipline, of traditional lit. crit., of clinical research. In a conference held in 1995 at the University of Paris VII, an established literary academic referred to *Lts* as a risky text, 'un texte risqué', a text effacing both the specificity of literature and the specificity of psychoanalysis.[14] This very interrogation is at the heart of Kristeva's transgressive, risk-taking yet ethical, activity. It is a deliberate exorbitance inseparable from her work as analyst in which nothing is outside the frame.

In a review of Kristeva's *Les nouvelles maladies de l'âme* Jacqueline Rose, responding to the significant way Kristeva inscribes subjectivity into her more recent writing, refers to parts of the Kristeva text as 'partial autobiography', crossing the traditional academic boundaries drawn around objectivity and subjectivity.[15] I myself in an article on Nerval's 'El Desdichado' have wondered about Kristeva's boundary crossing, for in her own essay on this poem she not only makes no distinction between the poetic subject and Nerval but juxtaposes fragments of discourse of different origin and status until we are unsure whether she is reading this poem as a literary critic, a clinician or as a lyrical poet.[16] This is subjectivity challenging the establishment, revolt in practice. It is a shock to those of us educated in the heydays of structuralism and post-structuralism, who learned to ignore biography, both the writer's and our own, when writing academic papers. Kristeva ignores neither and furthermore, she concludes the essay on Nerval with an interpretation of his suicide. I asked her about this. Wasn't suicide outside the frame of interpretation? Wasn't it even outside the frame of analytic interpretation? 'That is the wager', 'C'est le pari', she replied.

During this discussion I was struck by Kristeva's free-thinking yet always thoughtful exorbitance, by her commitment and optimism. I evoked her model of a 'monstrous intimacy', derived from the polymorphous

plasticity of Proust's text, as a transgressive challenge to
established codes of the strange and the familiar:

> Faites confiance aux monstres qui, à la traversée des
> langues et des esprits, à l'abri des écrans télévisés et dans
> le secret des pages, composent l'utopie d'une intimité
> polyphonique.[17]

> Have confidence in those monsters who, crossing
> between languages and minds, sheltered from television
> screens and inhabiting secret pages, make up the utopia
> of a polyphonic intimacy.

I commented upon the double nature – both exalting and
frightening – of this notion of monstruous intimacy. Where
are the symbolic limits? I asked. 'They are what is being
contested', she replied.

We might now see Kristeva's work as a whole in relation
to two fundamental projects: that of constituting an identity,
and that of speaking unspeakable truths, having confidence
in the monsters which inhabit our nightmares and fantasies.
Symbolising these monsters is tantamount to speaking
the unspeakable, representing the unrepresentable. In this
sense identity cannot then become fixed and totalitarian
but must remain open, mobile and tolerant of difference;
for accepting the difference in oneself, be this in the form
of strangeness, monstrosity, femininity or masculinity will
involve being tolerant of oneself – which is fundamental
to psychic health – and open to the alterity of the other,
which will check the reactionary activities of racism,
repression or misogyny. So both these involve negotiating
limits, shifting frontiers and shaping transgression.
Constituting an identity involves crossing boundaries: 'se
situer, parler, fragmenter et dissoudre l'enclos du propre
et de l'identique'[18] (situating oneself, speaking, breaking
out of the enclosures of propriety and sameness).

As far as speaking the unspeakable is concerned, we have
seen how in both literary and clinical research, Kristeva
pours her energy into showing how unspoken experience
may and does achieve representation. This is the
background to the theory of revolt, for any expression or
representation of the psychic reality of our fantasies and
imagination will transgress the symbolic, social or linguistic
code somewhere along the line. Such codes are necessary
and designed to keep the world of the imagination in
check. Yet different forms of revolt and revolution keep
them ripe for renewal. There is in oedipal identity a
libidinal drive to revolt against and be revolted with the
symbolic code, the law and taboo. Freud's account of the
Oedipus complex, and the revolt of the primal horde
against the father, the symbolic patricide at the foundation
of any society which forms the subject of 'Totem and
Taboo', inform Kristeva's reflection in *Snsr*:

> La tradition freudienne a l'avantage d'avoir mis en
> évidence le rôle structurant de l'Oedipe et du phallus.
> Mais elle a peut-être le désavantage de l'avoir fait sans
> pointer les formes de modification, de transgression,
> de révolte – pour employer le terme qui m'intéresse cette
> année – vis-à-vis de cet ordre.[19]

> The Freudian tradition has the advantage of having
> made manifest the structural importance of the Oedipus
> complex and of the phallus. But perhaps it has the
> disadvantage of having done that without pointing to
> the forms of modification, of transgression, of revolt
> ... which take place before the law of that order.

Man's capacity for revolt lies in his capacity to speak
and to create meaning: 'il organise un espace sacré,
s'élabore un culte de ce qui est, finalement, notre capacité
de signifier'.[20] (He organises a sacred space in which
he cultivates our capacity, a shared capacity, for
representation.)

But we must not forget the dimension transversal to man's capacity to create sacred and symbolic meaning, that is, the dimension of the pre-verbal, the semiotic, the archaic maternal space. It is this space, according to Kristeva, which holds the secret to an alternative fluidity, outside the binary logic organised by the phallus. It is worth commenting, nonetheless, that without the symbolic order, the maternal space itself constitutes a binary logic, a logic of infinite demand, which must be symbolised and represented again and again. The feminine economy of the maternal space must, for its own survival, be shaped by the symbolic framework of the law. A truly heterogeneous economy ignores neither the pre-verbal, fusional reality of mother/infant experience nor the importance of its symbolic interruption and framework.

> il est intéressant de se demander, eu égard à la prévalence du phallus, quelles seraient les autres logiques, différentes de la logique binaire, qu'organise le phallus. Est-ce dans cet écart qu'il est possible de penser le sémiotique, le préverbal, ainsi que toutes formes d'organisations fluides, sensorielles.[21]

It is interesting to ask, with regard to the prevalence of the phallus, what other systems might exist apart from the binary system organised by the phallus. Stepping outside binary logic enables us to think through the semiotic, the pre-verbal and other fluid, sensory forms of organisation.

What is most striking about Kristeva's recent work is that in her elaboration of the theory of revolt she is moving towards a model of oedipal identity which, going beyond Freud's model, is becoming increasingly differentiated, sexually. This will lead to a fascinating account of her theory of female oedipal identity which she calls *Oedipe-bis*. The chapter in *Snsr* entitled 'De l'étrangeté du phallus' ('On the Strangeness of the Phallus') encapsulates previous

observations on sexual difference and poses a pertinent
answer to her Anglo-American feminist critics who have
repeatedly bemoaned a lack of attention to sexual
difference. Is it not significant that Kristeva's thoughtful
and elaborate response which is in fact subtitled 'le féminin
entre illusion et désillusion' ('The Feminine between
Illusion and Disillusion'), has taken time and is the result
of clinical experience? Thought, like any oedipal activity,
is submitted to historical and sexual constraints. Freud
was submitted to historical and sexual constraints. He did
not fully understand his female patients. His theories are
the result of empirical, slowly-unfolding attempts at
therapeutic treatment. Kristeva has not jumped on the
bandwagon of sexual difference as separatism. She has
waited patiently for a model of female sexual identity to
emerge and unfold. This model has emerged from
experience, in the sense that she attributes to that term;
it is not the result of abstract theorising. I shall refer
further to Kristeva's essay on sexual difference in my final
chapter on femininity.

In *Snsr* Julia Kristeva examines the psychic and cultural
conditions of revolt. The first half of the book is an exposé
of the concept of rebellion which Freud elaborates in his
writing, of oedipal revolt against the symbolic father, the
revolt of the primal horde against the sacred pact, against
the prohibition of incest and phallic monism. The second
half of the book examines revolt in relation to three male
intellectual figures of modern France, Louis Aragon, Jean-
Paul Sartre and Roland Barthes. What these three figures
have in common is to have been brought up in the absence
of a father-figure. The possibility of oedipal revolt is for
them displaced in writing in the form of creative rebellion.
Revolt is to be understood here in its etymological sense,
previously evoked, in the sense of a movement, a return
to an instance of trauma, usually oedipal, in the process
of writing. There exist, of course, analogous processes of
displacement for this creative return, of which the optimal

model is psychoanalysis. The tense of this return and therefore the tense of both literary and psychoanalytic experience is a future anterior. In French, the future anterior is a future-perfect tense referring to a past seen in relation to some point in the future.

We see in Chapter 4, with regard to femininity, that an eternal irony inscribes woman in the possibility of revolt, an ironic distance from the symbolic order. Sartre's revolt takes the form of an oedipal revolt against his maternal grandfather, recounted in *Les mots*, and then the form of the melancholic structure which underlies his concept of nausea. Sartre's nausea, like Kristeva's abject, hovers between difference and sameness, between the limits of strangeness and foreignness. There is a valorisation of theatricality and the espousal of negativity as 'a nothingness at work' in literature, and finally a total form of political engagement which, according to Kristeva, leaves no possibility for psychic ressurrection.

Roland Barthes' revolt takes the form of a demystification of writing, of going beyond the apparent to uncover the ultra and infra-linguistic laws of language, that which lies both beyond and beneath. We can see how Barthes' enterprise has influenced Kristeva's here, how they share that preoccupation to speak the unspeakable, to reveal the body in the text, how Barthes' emphasis on the pleasure in the text and Kristeva's emphasis on the semiotic stem from the same preoccupation. In the same way, Kristeva's defence of structuralism, often referred to these days as a Terrorism of the Sign, is a defence of her own activity at that period. Kristeva insists that the structuralists of the 1970s and 1980s were dissidents from Marxism, thinkers who submitted Marxist doxa to structuralist scrutiny and their position was in fact a revolt against Marxist ideology as it was a revolt against all totalitarian discourse. In a forthcoming paper on Kristeva, Jonathan Rée remembers her reply to his question about the *Tel Quel* group's espousal of Maoism in this period: 'It was an archeology of Utopia.'[22] The term 'archeology' here corresponds to her notion of revolt as a return which is an interrogation in the future anterior tense. Reading Kristeva on Barthes we also see how her idea of the subject of writing as a subject in process, which is also the subject of sublimation, derives from semiology's de-hierarchisation of writing, and how in turn this focus on the signifying process involves the slow destructuring and re-elaboration of language which characterises a psychoanalysis. So, says Kristeva, writing for Barthes is none other than the realisation of that liberty which is realised when trauma has been traversed and inscribed in a certain law.[23]

In a recent review of *Snsr* in *Le Monde des livres* Michel Contat describes the impact of Kristeva's work in Kristevan terms:

> Le combat intellectuel de Kristeva, on le voit bien dans ce cours, est mené contre le cognitivisme qui prétend ne connaître de l'esprit que son rapport à la connaissance, c'est-à-dire à lui-même asexué, et non plus son rapport à l'autre, par le corps, les sens, l'affectivité. Son combat esthétique et moral, elle le mène contre les intégrismes qui nient la liberté, ses jouissances et ses jeux, et contre le nihilisme qui renforce l'impossible en renonçant à l'affronter par la littérature. C'est un beau combat qui appelle alliance, dans l'exacte mesure où il ne se déprend pas de l'ironie.[24]

Julia Kristeva's intellectual combat announces itself very clearly in these lectures, in this book, as a combat against cognitivism whose only conception of the mind lies in its relation to knowledge, that is in its own asexuality, and not in its relation to the other, through the body, meaning and affectivity. It is an aesthetic and moral combat against fundamentalism which denies the play and enjoyment of liberty, and against nihilism which reinforces the impossible by refusing its encounter with literature. It is a noble combat which calls for alliance in the same measure as it possesses an ironic reflexivity.

We may talk of an evident return to Freud in Kristeva's recent work. Her chapter 'Les métamorphoses du langage' in *Snsr*, traces Freud's changing topographies of the mind and their relation to language. This account of Freud's three topographies corresponds to the evolution of her own thinking about language. It begins with the idea of language as a heterogeneous construction, containing the verbal, crossed through by the sexual, and evolves towards an emphasis on the importance of language as intermediary and transitional, bringing the unrepresentable into words. Both Freud and Kristeva emphasise the importance of processes of identification and sublimation in verbalisation, and the thinking of each culminates in a reflection on language and Being, Freud's phylogenesis, Kristeva's theory of experience.

Earlier in this chapter I referred to a conference in which a representative of the French university literary establishment expressed shock at the way in which Kristeva collapses the particular boundaries of literature and psycho-analysis in *Le temps sensible*. The example cited was a passage in which Kristeva's insistence on the corporeality of Proust's text and its representation of perversion enables her to draw an analogy between reading Proust and treating the autistic child. This passage is about a particular kind of receptivity, an ability to receive impressions and sensations openly and without reactionary strongholds. It is about an enquiring openness to experience and to iden-tification which is ultimately both a source of self-knowledge and a capacity to understand otherness:

> La lecture de Proust suggère des figures capables de modeler la chair de nos identifications intenses avec ceux qui ne parlent ni ne pensent leurs sensations ... car par-delà le symptôme autiste de la caverne sensorielle, il s'agit d'une région frontalière de notre psychisme que

l'expérience esthétique remémore et où se ressource, sans s'y reduire, l'interprétation analytique elle-même.[25]

Reading Proust suggests to us figures of modelling the body of our intense identifications with those who neither speak nor think their sensations ... For beyond the autistic symptom of the sensorial cavern there is a psychic border-country which is remembered in aesthetic experience and where analytic interpretation finds its resources.

The intense sensoriality of autism is ineffable. It is that ultimate dissociation of the body from language, a psychic border-country which encapsulates Kristeva's concern from *La révolution du langage poétique* to *Le temps sensible*, that of pushing against boundaries and bringing the unspeakable into language.

CHAPTER 4

Foreignness, Femininity, Sacrifice

Femininity, or being female, has always been closely related to exile or foreignness in Kristeva. This is a theoretical structure in Kristeva's thought, which is of course, closely bound up with her biography. It is perhaps important here to recall some elements of that biography in their painful simplicity even if they enter into Kristeva's work in the form of sublimations – fictional or analytical ones. Julia Kristeva left her native country, Bulgaria, in 1965 with a doctoral fellowship to study in Paris. When she married Philippe Sollers and decided to stay she became in effect an Eastern European dissident, while – and this is crucial to her intellectual position – maintaining dissidence as a personal reality which also characterised her relation to France. In adopting the West she entered into a scenario of abandonment, abandonment of one's native country, abandonment by one's native country, and little ground for reconciliation, for visits home, until the fall of the Berlin Wall in 1989. The scenario is one with which we are familiar through all those Eastern Europeans who have chosen to cultivate their talents in the West and, given the political circumstances, it amounts to separation at its most brutal, which perhaps explains the powerful release of creative energy such figures seem to carry with them and the long work of mourning that creativity entails. With the death of her father as a result of a medical experiment in an East European hospital at the time of the fall of the Berlin Wall Kristeva's biography is stamped once again with a brutal reality and her work of mourning takes a fictional form in *Le viel homme et les loups*, a novel of enquiry, and an analytical and philosophical form in *Le temps sensible*, the work on Proust. The emotional, psychic and political reality of exile cannot be ignored here, nor can the enquiries into foreignness and femininity which sublimate that reality.

Kristeva permanently reiterates a sense of feeling foreign in France which is not unlike the sense of being a woman in the male order of things, of belonging and yet not quite fitting. Being a dissident, being foreign, being female, is what has enabled her to imagine and occupy that interrogative and exorbitant position which characterises her thought, to be at once outside and inside, to be seen as the quintessence of Frenchness abroad while feeling perfectly foreign at home, to be always in exile. And this state of exile, which is also a possibility for exorbitance, is one she has always related to being a woman.

In the essay 'Un nouveau type d'intellectuel, le dissident' ('A New Type of Intellectual, the Dissident'), which appeared in *Tel Quel* in 1977, Kristeva defines dissidence as a permanently alert, permanently fractious dismantling of totalising identities, a critical attitude from a position of exile which she relates to sexual difference:

> Et la différence sexuelle, les femmes: n'est-ce pas une autre dissidence? ... Trop prise par les frontières du corps et peut-être aussi de l'espèce, une femme se sent toujours en exil dans ces généralités qui font la commune mesure du consensus social, en même temps que par rapport au pouvoir de généralisation du langage. Cet éxil féminin, par rapport au Sens et au général, fait qu'une femme est toujours singulière.[1]

> And what of sexual difference, of women, are they not another dissidence? ... Too caught within the boundaries of the body and perhaps also of the species, a woman always feels exiled by those generalities which make up the just measure of social consensus, as she does in relation to language's generalising power. That exile

of the feminine in relation to Meaning and to generality, means that a woman is always different.

So woman is different, but feminism as a bid for difference cannot become a naïve argument for identity. Like the foreigner, the woman must construct an identity within the cultural and linguistic laws needed to argue that identity, and from which she, like the foreigner, will always feel partly estranged. For Kristeva, unlike feminists such as Beauvoir, femininity, like foreignness, is an inalienable difference. The woman intellectual's role in politics is then an imaginative one. It involves her imagination of a place for women and foreigners.

We have seen that in Kristeva, female identity involves negotiating one's identification with and difference from one's maternal origins and experiencing as strange or foreign all that is outside the maternal continent: that is language, the father, the law. We shall see how Kristeva elaborates this notion of strangeness in femininity in 'De l'étrangeté du phallus', the chapter on female sexual identity in *Snsr*. But first let us see how this transposes itself into actually being in exile.

In *Etrangers à nous-mêmes* (*Enm*) she relates foreignness to losing one's native, maternal language:

> Ne pas parler sa langue maternelle. Habiter des sonorités, des logiques coupées de la mémoire nocturne du corps, du sommeil aigre-doux de l'enfance. Porter en soi comme un caveau secret ... [2]

> To not speak one's native language. To inhabit sonorities and arguments cut off from the body's nocturnal memory, from the bitter-sweet sleep of childhood. To carry inside oneself something like a secret burial vault ...

The language here is reminiscent of the *caveau secret* of melancholy I discussed in Chapter 2 in relation to Kristeva's

work and the literary text *Eugénie Grandet*, of the refusal
to mourn the lost object.

What *Enm* is arguing is that the refusal of otherness, such
as racial intolerance, is born of the refusal to recognise one's
own otherness, to recognise and integrate the strangeness
in oneself. This is a compelling and fertile thesis which
enlightens issues of cultural, political and sexual difference
in the same measure as it explains a given society's response
to mental illness and different forms of madness or alterity.
But Kristeva is also talking about her own foreignness in
this text. It is a subjective, violent and painful text in
which the intellectual argument is stamped with personal
experience. This aspect of the text has gone largely
uncommented but it is impossible to ignore the internal
struggle which inhabits its language. I think it is important
to emphasise Kristeva's foreignness not only because she
insists upon repeating that it is something she experiences
as an everyday reality in France, but because it represents
a difficult separation, tantamount to a girl's separation from
her mother, and only recently does she turn or return to
this in her work. We could see the recent text 'Bulgarie,
ma souffrance' ('Bulgaria, My Suffering') as an attempt
to both mourn and remember the lost mother-tongue, the
maternal continent, and a text which could be seen as its
sequel, 'L'autre langue, ou traduire le sensible' ('The
Other Language, or Translating the Sensible'), as an
attempt to inscribe this mourning and remembering within
the parameters of the adopted country. 'Bulgarie, ma
souffrance', published in the summer of 1995, is the first
time Kristeva has written about Bulgaria in thirty years.
The previous resistance to do so must attest to a difficult,
in the sense of a melancholic or a violent, separation. It
is a personal attempt to bridge the gap, cross boundaries
and identify, in a text that has been published in Bulgarian
and in French, with Bulgaria's suffering. Yet it is not a
work of mourning since no loss has been completed:

Je n'ai pas perdu ma langue maternelle ... Je n'ai pas fait le deuil de la langue infantile au sens où un deuil 'accompli' serait un détachement, une cicatrice, voire un oubli.[3]

I have not lost my mother-tongue ... I have not mourned the language of infancy in the sense in which an 'accomplished' mourning would be a detachment, a scar, a forgetting ...

For can an exile ever accomplish the mourning for her native country if that native country has not been lost, if she is still inhabited by the presence of what she has left behind? There is then little expression of loss here, rather an expression of exile as transcendence, or rather of the spiritual sublimation of suffering which can take place *in* and *through* a foreign language:

Mais par-dessus cette crypte enfouie, sur ce reservoir stagnant qui croupit et se délite, j'ai bati une nouvelle demeure que j'habite et qui m'habite, et dans laquelle se déroule ce qu'on pourrait appeler, non sans prétention évidemment, la vraie vie de l'esprit et de la chair ... De ce flou qu'est mon immersion dans l'Etre ... je retiens une sonorité ponctuée de mots français.[4]

But on top of that buried crypt, that stagnant reservoir, festering and decomposing, I have built a new house which I inhabit and which inhabits me and in which there takes place what we could call, not without obvious pretention that is, the true life of the spirit and the flesh ... From the midst of my immersion in Being ... I retain a serenity punctuated by French words.

Il y a du matricide dans l'abandon d'une langue natale ... Destin toujours douloureux, l'exil est la seule voie qui nous reste ...[5]

> We can talk of matricide in the abandonment of a maternal tongue ... Exile, always a painful destiny, is the only path open to us ...

There is ambivalence in this simultaneous expression of transcendence or sublimation and suffering. The native language cannot be completely mourned in the sense that it has not been completely lost, but it has been partially lost and there must be a partial mourning. Kristeva is saying that exile is both sublimatory – in the sense that loss leads to creation on another level, and painful nonetheless. This is something she has reiterated in interviews, such as the one published in *Le Monde* in May 1996, which perhaps point to the injuries which line the path of exile for many: 'Je suis profondément quelqu'un de meurtri'/'deep-down I am a bruised and battered person', or in the *Times Higher Educational Supplement* in August 1994, 'I am in a good position to know what "foreignness" is all about. France is a very xenophobic country and the French see me as someone with a touch of the tarbrush trying to make it in their patch. Also the fact that I am a woman putting out unconventional ideas is something that upsets people in itself. Being Madame Philippe Sollers is also a source of conflict. So I feel uncomfortable here and, whenever I can, I take off to other countries. And this is where the paradox lies: in other countries, I find myself considered the quintessence of Frenchness.'[6]

So exile seems to involve the constant work of sublimating suffering, and in the text 'Bulgarie, ma souffrance' this suffering is related to separation from the maternal continent, mother and country. Yet in the later text, 'L'autre langue, ou traduire le sensible' published in the spring of 1997, after noting that the French word *souffrance* contains the suffix *France*, Kristeva elaborates the suffering of exile in relation to the fatherland. Exile, like femininity, seems to be destined to a play of irresolution and solution, moments of bliss, moments of pain and a constant renegotiation of frontiers in which nostalgia and estrangement switch place as the subject moves between countries. In this paradigm, the country of origin is the motherland, the mother, from whom a symbolic separation must be achieved, and the adopted country is the father, difficult, rigorous and alienating in his strangeness, to the girl-child; yet structured and therefore reassuring. France and its hard structures rescues Kristeva from the troubled black sea of Bulgarian nostalgia.

In the French language she insists upon the importance of the sensible, the importance of remembering the archaic past in one's language of adoption. This remembering is a translation of long-forgotten memories and she uses the language of Proust as a model for this time-consuming, difficult enterprise:

> ...même autochtone, l'écrivain ne cesse d'être un traducteur de ses passions dérobées, que la langue fondamentale qu'il se plait à traduire est la langue du sensible. Et que cet innomable fondement, cette rumeur de nos fibres et de nos rêves, ne se laisse jamais entièrement résorber, jamais réduire dans les codes des écoles, des clans, des institutions, des médias ...[7]

> ... even the writer who writes in his native language is a ceaseless translator of his secret passions; the fundamental language he translates is the language of the sensible. And that unnameable foundation, the distant sound coming from our dreams and the fibre of our bodies will never be completely reabsorbed, nor is it reducible to the codes of schools of thought, clans, institutions, the media.

The language of involuntary memory is a revolution, in the sense of a return to the latent music of the past. Kristeva quotes Baudelaire, 'le parfum de la terre natale', the perfume of the nativeland, the unspeakable of ancient mysterious affinities which remain to be translated. The inscription of the infantile in culture, of the semiotic in the symbolic, of the poetic in the literary text encapsulates her notion of *experience*, whereby intimacy is given a form and shared. This brings us to the notion of the text as an experience appealing at once to reason, the imagination and the unconscious and to language as a heterogeneous construction from which the intimacy of femininity is not excluded. The argument is developed in the latest volume of *Pouvoirs et limites de la psychanalyse, La révolte intime* (1997).[8]

I think if we draw together and moderate Kristeva's various elaborations of femininity, the picture which emerges involves shifting flexibly between different levels of illusion.

   In Kristeva's early work femininity is not a sexually specific category but rather construed linguistically and closely related to the transgressive, negative aspects of language which characterise the semiotic. It is here conceived as a realm of identity available to either sex. In Kristeva's work in the 1970s, references to femininity are conflated with writing on motherhood and the maternal. As we saw in Chapter 2 this disconcerted Kristeva's feminist critics. I would argue that at this time Kristeva was not ready to begin articulating female specificity as such but more concerned with tracing the topography of the pre-oedipal, maternal relationship in which the infant perceives the mother as total. She described its fusional bliss, cruelty and complacency and the transposition of this fusional experience, which particularly characterises mother/daughter relationships, onto relationships between women, such as we see in 'Stabat Mater'. In this text the woman's attempt at separation from the figure of the mother, from other women, leads to expressions of violence, hatred or withdrawal:

... lorsque l'autre femme se pose comme telle, c'est-à-
dire comme singulière et forcément en s'opposant, 'je'
suis saisie au point que 'je' n'y suis plus ... je lui tourne
amicalement le dos ... je m'acharne contre sa prétention
... je ne trouve de répit que dans l'éternel retour des
coups de haine.[9]

When the other woman presents herself as such, that
is as singular and in opposition, 'I' am struck to the point
that 'I' am no longer there ... I amicably turn away ...
I fight her pretentiousness ... My only respite is in the
infinite return of blows of strength, blows of hatred.

The 'I' is in inverted commas. It represents the female
subject, and the text represents the difficulty women have
in achieving separateness from other women without
conflict and difficulty.

More recently Kristeva's emphasis on singularity
underlines her attempt to elaborate the question of female
identity as individual and non-identical and to encourage
the important work of separation and differentiation this
involves. As Kristeva begins to write regularly about her
clinical experience in the 1980s (*Sn, Lnma*), there is a
concentration upon the actual difficulties of oedipal
identity, that is, of achieving a healthy separation from the
mother, for the girl-child, for women. Identifying to some
degree with her female patients here leads her to develop
a more moderate, differentiated model of female identity
while nonetheless maintaining the focus on singularity. She
focuses upon the particularities of female depression (*Sn*),
or, in essays on Mme de Staël and Hélène Deutsch, upon
the woman intellectual's particular struggles with
subjectivity and identity (*Lnma*). In a discussion with the
writer Danielle Sallenave, published in *L'Infini* in 1996,
Kristeva puts into perspective her emphasis on singularity
and its relation to female experience:

C'est cette singularité qui me paraît la plus précieuse
à développer à l'heure actuelle, et j'essaie de le faire avec
mes étudiantes, mes analysantes. Il y a plusieurs années,
j'avais fait un entretien avec des féministes belges des
Cahiers du Grif, que j'avais intitulé 'Unes femmes' – un
singulier au pluriel, pour mettre en valeur la solitude
d'une femme, et elle est essentielle; mais aussi pour
essayer de préserver la singularité de chaque femme pour
qu'elle ne disparaîsse pas dans quelque 'cause
commune' que ce soit.[10]

It is that singularity which strikes me as having the most
precious potential at the present time, and I try to
encourage it in my female students and analysands.
Several years ago I gave an interview to the Belgian
feminists at the *Cahiers du Grif* and I called my piece
'Unes femmes' – a singular in the plural, in order to
draw attention to women's solitude and its vital
importance, but also in an attempt to preserve the
singularity of each woman and to prevent it being
swallowed up by the common cause.

I think this emphasis on singularity gives the measure of
Kristeva's feminism both in so far as it promotes the idea
of individual identity and fulfilment and in as much as it
resists therefore notions of solidarity or corporate identity.
In November 1996 Julia Kristeva's seminar at Paris VII
opened the second volume of her work on the *Powers and
Limits of Psychoanalysis* of which *Snsr* constituted the first
volume and *La révolte intime* (May 1997) the second. The
seminar is entitled 'Le génie féminin' ('Female Genius'
or 'Genius in the Feminine') and focuses upon the figure
of Hannah Arendt. Kristeva is concerned with addressing
the question of what distinguishes women's contribution
to psychoanalysis and the human sciences in the twentieth
century; how women define and embody their identification
with and revolt against the symbolic order, and what
characterises their answers, in psychoanalysis, literature

and philosophy, to the pain and loss of meaning which characterise times of distress at a personal and national level. We can place Kristeva's work on Hannah Arendt in the light of these reflections on foreignness and femininity embodied in the figure of Hannah Arendt herself and evidenced in her political imagination. Indeed Kristeva's work on Hannah Arendt seems to mark a manifest return to politics, a new enquiry into the old questions of exile and femininity through biography, as it also marks Kristeva's first biography and first major work on a woman thinker with whose story she identifies.

In *Sn* and *Lnma* Kristeva tries to return to and open up what both Freud and Lacan sensed as a forbidding hermetic area – female sexuality. Her insistence on the pre-oedipal, ineffable – semiotic – infrastructure to femininity is reminiscent of Lacan's definition of femininity as that which cannot be represented. But Kristeva wants to achieve some sort of representation and verbalisation of the unrepresentable, 'dark continent'. This is a constant preoccupation in her work and the stamp of her originality. She affirms that women's sexual identity, their foothold in the symbolic, in language, society and culture is difficult and precarious. The woman must constantly recreate forms of identification with the socio-cultural order, the law of the father, against the background of the demands of her own body, of maternal attention, the desire for a child, as well as her identification with and desire for her own sex, the allure of sameness. She must constantly reconstruct her own oedipal position which rests upon her identification with her mother's desire for someone other than the child, a third party. There will always be some relinquishment of female identity in integrated femininity as there is a relinquishment of the maternal body, for the woman, in heterosexual seduction. Thus any sexuality is a configuration in the same individual of feminine and masculine. Kristeva elaborates a picture of female identity in which individuation is set against the demands of

procreativity as well as constantly interacting with the
allure of sameness – or homosexual desire, and in which
heterosexuality implies a more or less successful
transcendence of homosexual fixation. There is a
perceptible Freudian emphasis here upon sexual identity
as adaptive to biology. For Kristeva, the woman's revolt
relates to the depression which accompanies the
impossibility and melancholy of maternal fixation in the
abject position or, conversely, to the exhaustion of too great
an investment in phallic identity. In the abject position,
as we see in Chapter 2, the woman, disappointed or
unable to identify with the symbolic order, returns to an
undifferentiated relationship with the maternal body.
Alternatively, but no more liberating, there is an aspect
of female identity in which the woman or 'superwoman'
falls prey to the exhaustion or potential alienation of too
great an investment in phallic identity and suffers from
her alienation from the feminine, as indeed do men who
overinvest the symbolic. Such pitfalls of female identity
are described in 'De l'étrangeté du phallus' in *Snsr*.
Opening this chapter on female oedipal identity Kristeva
cites Freud's 'Female Sexuality':

> ... there can be no doubt that the bisexuality, which is
> present, as we believe, in the innate disposition of
> human beings, comes to the fore much more clearly
> in women than in men.[11]

In accordance with this model Kristeva elaborates her
own definition of femininity in which the archaic
mother–daughter relationship encapsulates that semiotic,
sensory realm which we can designate as a primary
homosexuality and which can be seen as an endogenous
layer of femininity in general. In *Lts* primary homosexuality
is seen as constitutive of female sexuality in this way.
Here Kristeva examines Proust's representation of female
homosexuality, through the figure of Albertine, as a representation of 'les jeunes filles en fleur'. A plastic pictorial

whirlwind of light and colour, a voluptuous fusional state of feminine non-differentiation represents a homosexual layer of femininity with which the writer identifies and thus he depicts his own femininity. Such an openness to femininity as that manifest by the narrator of Proust's text is, for Kristeva, as she argues with relation to Aragon, Sartre and Barthes in *Snsr*, an openness to singularity and questioning for either sex. Kristeva's male examples share the ironic secret of femininity in their poetic, philosophical and semiotic questioning of the symbolic. Aragon's writing is at one and the same time opposed to action and to art. There is in Surrealism a cult of the feminine which Aragon lives out in his legendary relationship with Elsa Triolet, his poetic and political partner, his muse and fellow-communist. His political engagements have a theatrical value, argues Kristeva, in that he is both an aristocrat and a stalinist.

In Kristeva's model of sexuality, masculinity is synonymous with the fixed identities and laws of the symbolic. As such it is a guarantor of the social order as well as of the scene of heterosexual seduction. As Kristeva will show in 'De l'étrangeté du phallus', it is when the symbolic fails a woman, when her lovelife or professional life falters, that she is open to the estrangement and marginality of her condition, to her precarious footing in the strangeness of the phallic, named so because governed by the symbol of the phallus. In the interview with Danielle Sallenave mentioned above, Kristeva compares this strangeness which characterises how a woman feels in the social community, to Hegel's definition of femininity as 'the eternal irony of the community', 'l'éternelle ironie de la communauté':

> Car s'il est vrai que la féminité est une étrangeté, une 'ironie de la communauté' (Hegel), elle devrait pouvoir marquer sa solidarité avec les autres formes d'étrangeté et de marginalité dans le monde moderne.[12]

> If it were true that femininity is a strangeness, an 'irony of the community' (Hegel), the woman should be able to make manifest her solidarity with other forms of strangeness and marginality in the modern world.

She seems to be saying 'Let us tap the resources of this marginality and strangeness which constitutes femininity', and there is a suggestion, when she talks about future writing projects, of the forms this might take such as a feminine economy of time as developed in the thinking of Hannah Arendt.

The focus on women's experience announced in 'De l'étrangeté du phallus' is certainly fundamental to future work. It also announces a return to and elaboration of previous thinking such as the idea of a specific female temporality which she defined in 'Le temps des femmes'/ 'Women's Time'. 'Le temps des femmes' was published in 1979 and forms the final chapter of *Lnma* (1993). Here she talks about two generations of feminists, the first belonging to cursive, linear history, the generation of feminists who fought for equality with men, and a second generation who argued for difference or female specificity and whom we can see as belonging to monumental, cyclical time. If we look at each generation in terms of a battle for identity, of finding a language to represent subjectivity and to breach the separations and absences which threaten that identity we can see how a clinical paradigm emerges. The first generation attempts to master these things in a way that corresponds to typical masculinity, mastery, control, the linear time of the obsessional; whereas the second generation marks a refusal to identify with a male order, a denial, a pull towards the corporeality and silences of total feminine subjectivity, the cyclical time, the temporal dissociations of the hysteric. This is a rejection of patriarchy and the law of the father. But neither order can survive as a totality. The argument of 'Women's Time' is that from the two generations of feminists defined might emerge a new generation of women who can break out of the binary logic of inclusion – linear obsessional time, or exclusion – hysterical, cyclical time, from the male order. This new generation might recognise the socio-symbolic contract as necessarily sacrificial for all individuals and as always involving a necessary relinquishment of total identity, be that sexual, national, economic or religious. This third generation will correspond to a free, fluid form of subjectivity able to integrate separation and difference. As Kristeva argued in 'Il n'y a pas de maître à langage' (1979), the inscription of the feminine in the masculine is the key to a vital heterogeneity. The argument of this text might be resumed as follows: the feminine is what inscribes heterogeneity in language. It has to be inscribed in the order of language to have an existence. To make the feminine a challenge to or denial of the laws of the symbolic is to relegate the feminine to the ineffable. There is no mastery in language, there is just a vital heterogeneity: the order of signification submitted to the transgressions, metaphors, metonymies, intonation, alliteration, sonority and accents of the pre-verbal semiotic. This is the vital heterogeneity of a fluid free subjectivity and a heterosexual social contract, each built upon the capacity to contain sacrifice.

Paradigm for Femininity

In 'De l'étrangeté du phallus', whose subtitle translates as 'The Feminine between Illusion and Disillusion', Kristeva proposes her most differentiated model of female sexuality and elaborates what she calls *Oedipe-bis*, the girl's Oedipus complex B.[13] *Bis*, in French, implies the same again, like *encore*, and once removed, like second in second cousin. The girl's Oedipus complex B involves a double displacement. In the Freudian Oedipus complex the boy overcomes incestuous desire for the mother through identifying with the father as at once a castrating prohibition and a loving figure who, as a figure for the child's processes of identification, will enable the boy to displace desire onto other women. Desire undergoes prohibition and displacement, but it is the same desire nonetheless, that of male for female. It is not difficult to see how the girl's Oedipus complex involves both prohibition, displacement, *and* a change of object. For the girl too the mother is the first seductress; her desire is prohibited by the father-figure or by the mother's desire for a person other than the child: it must be displaced and it must change object. She will identify with the mother's desire for the father. But unlike the boy she cannot transpose her primal relationship with and desire for the mother's body into heterosexual relationships. She is caught between the sensible and the signifier, required to desire a strange, illusory, masculine order signified by the phallus. The pre-oedipal relation with the mother's body then becomes a partially repressed layer of her sexuality, a sensory secret which Kristeva relates to memories too distant to be recalled, but which are rather hallucinated. These secret memories are the key to her survival in the strange, illusory order of the phallus.

It is a compelling hypothesis, a theory which enables women to be what Kristeva calls psychically bisexual, that is to be able to feel estranged from masculinity and nostalgic for femininity, to live out that nostalgia in their femininity, in motherhood, in female friendships and to submit that strangeness to the scene, the game, of heterosexual seduction. This survival kit saves them from both total submission to or appropriation of the masculine *and* from fusional, non-differentiated female relationships, to move between the feminine and the masculine. It is movement between the feminine and the masculine, a delicate, difficult configuration, a fantasy to remedy other less liveable fantasies.

Here I propose my own translations of a selection of key passages from this yet untranslated essay, published in May 1996. The book *Sens et non-sens de la révolte* is the transcript of Kristeva's weekly post-graduate seminar held at Jussieu, the University of Paris VII in the academic year 1994–95. It is Kristeva live, addressing, including and motivating her student-interlocutors. The thinking is at once didactic, interrogative, personal and reflective:

> Like all successes, female psychical bisexuality is certainly a fantasy. It supposes the inscription of female subjectivity in the signifying, phallic order, along with the procession of pleasures and symbolic gratifications ([*Oedipe-prime*] the oedipal) afforded by that strange illusory order; it also supposes the displacement of castration, of depression and of sexual depreciation in a revalorisation of the maternal and consequently feminine role and this happens through a reconciliation with primary homosexuality; it finally implies the investment of the real presence of the phallus-child, who is a less illusory living proof of triumph over castration – even if always already somewhat 'estranged'. In that undeniable vortex formed by the attachment to and detachment from the phallus (the signifier, desire), female bisexuality is no more or no less than an experience of sense and its gestation, of language and its erosion, of being and its reserve.[14]

> You will have understood, that I see in the psychical bisexuality of the woman not a cult of the phallus, or a going beyond it, even less a being within it, but a maintaining and an 'estrangement' of illusion as illusion.[15]

> I leave you contemplating the immeasurable psychical effort required to accede to that psychically bisexual being which is woman, a being who never adheres to the illusion of being, no more than to the being of that illusion itself.[16]

In this model, being psychically bisexual, being a woman, involves a partial estrangement from the illusory order of discourse. The woman nonetheless espouses this order and puts it at the service of her imagination while remaining attached to the nostalgia of maternal presence embodied in her sensory relationship with the child. She must in turn initiate the child into the illusory order of language which is at once the source of her disillusionment and the cloth which she will line with her losses. Few thinkers have modelled such a viable paradigm for femininity, delicately moderating the woman's investment in language, the imagination and her body.

Conclusion

If this conclusion were to have a title like the other chapters and to reflect Julia Kristeva's thinking at the time of writing I might call it 'The Intimate, the Imaginary and Discourse'. Kristeva's reflections on the intimate refer to experience at its most internal and profound, to a coalescence of sensory and spiritual experience which traverses religious and philosophical thought from Saint Augustin and Loyola, through Kant and Freud, binding together the notions of life and language which are so important in Kristeva's work.[1] The emphasis on the imaginary recoups phenomenology's idea of negativity, which Merleau-Ponty calls non-being and Sartre, nothingness; the image is fundamentally negative as it makes absence present. The objects of psychoanalysis are these psychical representations of absence, of things and experiences which, for one reason or another, remain lost or unrealised and which in the time-consuming language of literature and psychoanalysis are liberated into consciousness and into an economy of desire. Kristeva insists upon the inalienable importance of this negative economy of the imaginary as much as she insists that it must never be total, but rather inscribed in discourse, embracing the material reality of the other, of history, of politics. Western society today is trapped in an image-bound popular culture, producing and consuming one image after another with little time or space for verbalisation. In this context the image is standardised and lifeless. Furthermore the globalisation of the economy and of systems of communication we are all experiencing in everyday life leaves our individual experience prey to virtual reality, and it is no surprise that such a threat creates reactionary battles for identity, and on a wider political scale, forms of fundamentalism or ethnic grouping. This of course is no answer. Our only hope is to hang onto a sense of history, both personal and social, and to insist upon the creation of a time and place in language, in culture, for the experience and processing of the sensible, the intimate, the imaginary – to remember a more or less long-forgotten period of our personal experience – our infancy.

We have seen that this apparent regression to a pre-verbal, infantile state of being involves a return to the poetic foundations of language as well as a revolt against the stasis of nostalgia in the form of a questioning and displacement of the past, a revolution in time which, as it advances inexorably foward, for the individual and society, must stand still and expand to incorporate that timelessness which is integral to spiritual and cultural experience. In today's more or less secular society, cultural activity has therefore a crucial sublimatory function. I have called this account of Kristeva's work *Speaking the Unspeakable* in order to draw attention to her investment in the sublimatory powers of cultural activity for the individual and for society at large. For language will always speak the unspeakable as the unconscious will make itself known. And language which reserves a place for the imaginary will achieve representations of that unspeakability. The silences will become an issue. There are unspeakable areas in our personal and collective past and any analyst knows that silence is part of survival and must be broken gently and never totally. Bringing the silences of the past or of the unconscious into language is a delicate activity. Primo Levi said of the Holocaust that the silence is part of the survival. Those very words take their place in the memory of the Holocaust and his suicide attests to the difficulty of breaking silence. Yet the unspeakable will be spoken. The dissident voices of literature, psychoanalysis and intellectual enquiry occupy that delicate time and space in which unspeakability may and does find representation and which encapsulates the work of Julia Kristeva. The evolution of that work represents Julia Kristeva's sublimation of her own personal history and experience as much as it represents a progressive alliance of the personal and the intellectual in the form of enquiries into maternal, analytic and literary experience, into foreignness and femininity. This bringing the personal into the intellectual reflects her passionate demand for a certain kind of truth, or activity of truth which will never be complete, and that demand, both personal and collective, is that thought resemble life as closely and openly as possible:

> Si nous ne mettions pas sans cesse à vif l'étrangeté de notre vie intime pour la transposer à nouveau dans d'autres signes, aurions-nous une vie psychique, serions-nous des êtres vivants?[2]

> If we did not ceaselessly expose the strangeness of our internal life – and transpose it ceaselessly into other signs, would there be a life of the psyche, would we be living beings?

Notes

Introduction

1. Interview, Julia Kristeva and Danielle Sallenave, 1994–95, 'L'expérience littéraire est-elle encore possible?', *L'Infini* 53 (Spring 1996), p. 20. This translation and all following translations are my own.
2. Ibid., p. 39.
3. See Josyane Savigneau, 'Julia Kristeva et ses mystères', *Le Monde*, 31 May 1996.
4. For references, see Bibliography.
5. I refer particularly to Leslie Hill's 'Julia Kristeva' in John Fletcher and Andrew Benjamin (eds), *Abjection, Melancholia and Love: The Work of Julia Kristeva* (London: Routledge 1990), pp. 137–56.
6. Kelly Oliver, *Reading Kristeva* (New York: Routledge 1993); Anna Smith, *Julia Kristeva: Readings of Exile and Estrangement* (London and Basingstoke: Macmillan 1996).
7. Julia Kristeva, 'Monstrueuse intimité (De la littérature comme expérience)', *L'Infini* 48 (Winter 1994), p. 60 (paper given at the Nobel Symposium, August 1994).
8. Anne-Marie Smith (ed.), *Powers of Transgression/Julia Kristeva*, special issue of *Paragraph*, vol. 20, no. 3, November 1997.
9. Patrick Ffrench, *The Time of Theory: A History of Tel Quel 1960–83* (Oxford: Oxford University Press 1995); Philippe Forest, *Histoire de Tel Quel* (Paris: Seuil 1995).

Chapter 1

1. Bice Benvenuto and Roger Kennedy, *The Works of Jacques Lacan: An Introduction* (London: Free Association Books 1986).
2. John Lechte, *Julia Kristeva* (London: Routledge 1990).
3. Julia Kristeva, *La révolution du langage poétique* (Paris: Seuil 1974), p. 612.
4. Ibid., pp. 223–6.
5. Ibid., p. 22.
6. James Joyce, 'The Dead' (1907), in *Dubliners* (Harmondsworth: Penguin Books 1956).
7. Kristeva, *Lrlp*, p. 161.
8. Julia Kristeva, 'Il n'y a pas de maître à langage', *Nouvelle revue de psychanalyse* 20 (Autumn 1979), p. 134.
9. Julia Kristeva, 'Les nouvelles maladies de l'âme', *L'Infini* 45 (Spring 1994), p. 73.
10. Joyce, 'The Dead', p. 207.
11. Ibid; *The Dead*, John Huston, Zenith productions, Liffey Films 1987.
12. Julia Kristeva, *Pouvoirs de l'horreur: Essai sur l'abjection* (Paris: Seuil 1980), p. 15.

Chapter 2

1. Julia Kristeva, 'Stabat Mater' in *Histoires d'amour* (Paris: Denoel 1983), p. 303.
2. Ibid., p. 317.
3. Ibid., p. 318.
4. Ibid., p. 320.
5. John Lechte, 'Horror, Love, Melancholy' in Lechte, *Julia Kristeva*, pp. 157–98.
6. Anna Smith, 'A Reversible Space: the Essence of Ambassadorship' in Anne-Marie Smith (ed.), *Powers of Transgression*, special issue of *Paragraph*.

7. John Fletcher and Andrew Benjamin (eds), *Abjection, Melancholia and Love: The Work of Julia Kristeva* (London: Routledge 1990).
8. Elizabeth Gross, 'The Body of Signification', pp. 80–103.
9. Noreen O'Connor, 'The An-arche of Psychotherapy', pp. 42–52.
10. Sigmund Freud, 'Leonardo da Vinci and a Memory of his Childhood' (1910), in James Strachey (ed.), Standard Edition, II (London: Hogarth Press 1959).
11. Nicolas Abraham and Maria Torok, 'Deuil ou mélancolie' in *L'Ecorce et le noyau* (Paris: Aubier-Flammarion 1978), pp. 259–74.
12. Julia Kristeva, 'Nerval, El Desdichado' in Julia Kristeva, *Soleil noir, dépression et mélancholie* (Paris: Gallimard 1987), pp. 152–82.
13. Anne-Marie Smith, '"El Desdichado": Vocal Gesture and Transference in the Melancholic text', *Paragraph*, vol. 19, no. 1, March 1996, pp. 49–57.
14. Julia Kristeva, 'Dépression et dépressivité', lecture at the Société Psychanalytique de Paris, 11 March 1993.
15. *The Penguin Book of French Verse: The Nineteenth Century*, (ed.) Anthony Hartley (1957).
16. Julia Kristeva, 'Figures de la dépression féminine', *Soleil noir, dépression et mélancolie*, pp. 79–97.
17. Anne-Marie Smith, '"Le texte de la vie des femmes": Female Melancholia in Eugénie Grandet', *Nottingham French Studies*, vol. 35, no. 2, Autumn 1996.
18. Kristeva, 'Figures de la dépression féminine', p. 101.
19. Luce Irigaray, *Speculum de l'autre femme* (Paris: Minuit 1974). For a critical analysis of Irigaray on female melancholia, see Margaret Whitford, *Luce Irigaray: Philosophy in the Feminine* (London: Routledge 1991).

Chapter 3

1. Julia Kristeva, *Histoires d'amour*, p. 16.
2. Ibid., p. 17.
3. Ibid., p. 48.

4. Kristeva, 'Les nouvelles maladies de l'âme', pp. 67–73.
5. Ibid., p. 71.
6. Ibid., p. 70.
7. Ibid., p. 71.
8. Kristeva, 'Les nouvelles maladies de l'âme', p. 165.
9. Ibid., p. 72.
10. Sigmund Freud, 'Female Sexuality'(1931), in *On Sexuality* (Harmondsworth: Pelican Books 1977), p. 372.
11. Kristeva, 'Monstrueuse intimité', p. 59.
12. Julia Kristeva, 'Quelle révolte aujourd'hui ?', *Sens et non-sens de la revolte* (Paris: Fayard 1996), pp. 7–46.
13. Sigmund Freud, 'Creative Writers and Daydreaming' (1908), in James Strachey (ed.), Standard Edition, IX (London: Hogarth Press 1959).
14. Josette Pacaly, 'D'un nouveau rapport à l'oeuvre littéraire chez le psychanalyste (Didier Anzieu et Julia Kristeva avec Beckett et Proust)', 'Psychanalyse et écriture de soi', conference, Université de Paris VII, 30 September 1995.
15. Jacqueline Rose, 'Fleshly Memories', *Times Literary Supplement*, 29 October 1993.
16. Anne-Marie Smith, '"El Desdichado": Vocal Gesture and Transference in the Melancholic Text', *Paragraph*, Vol. 19, no. 1, March 1996, pp. 49–57.
17. Kristeva, 'Monstrueuse intimité', p. 61.
18. Seminar entitled 'Sens et non-sens de la révolte', University of Paris VII, 28 November 1995.
19. Kristeva, *Sens et non-sens de la révolte*, p.186.
20. Ibid., p. 188.
21. Ibid.
22. Jonathan Rée, 'Revolutionary Archeology: Julia Kristeva and the Utopia of the Text' in Anne-Marie Smith (ed.) *Powers of Transgression*, p. 267.
23. Julia Kristeva, 'Roland Barthes et l'écriture', *Snsr*, p. 404.
24. Michel Contat, 'Le temps de la révolte', *Le monde des livres*, 31 May 1996.

25. Julia Kristeva, 'La sensation est-elle un langage?', *Le temps sensible*, pp. 305–6.

Chapter 4

1. Julia Kristeva, 'Un nouveau type d'intellectuel: le dissident', *Tel Quel* 74 (Winter 1977), p. 7.
2. Julia Kristeva, 'Le silence des polyglottes', *Etrangers à nous-mêmes*, pp. 26–7.
3. Julia Kristeva, 'Bulgarie, ma souffrance', *L'Infini* 49 (Spring 1995), p. 42.
4. Ibid.
5. Ibid., p. 44.
6. Julia Kristeva, 'From Couch to Conflict', *Times Higher Educational Supplement*, 19 August 1994, p. 17.
7. Julia Kristeva, 'L'autre langue ou traduire le sensible', *L'Infini* 57 (Spring 1997), p. 20.
8. Julia Kristeva, *La révolte intime: Pouvoirs et Limites de la Psychanalyse II* (Paris: Fayard 1997).
9. Kristeva, 'Stabat Mater', p. 321.
10. Kristeva, 'L'Expérience littéraire est-elle encore possible?', p. 46.
11. Freud, 'Female Sexuality' (1931), p. 374.
12. Kristeva, 'L'Expérience littéraire est-elle encore possible?', p. 46.
13. Kristeva, 'De l'étrangeté du phallus...', *Snsr*, p. 221.
14. Ibid., p. 220.
15. Ibid., p. 222.
16. Ibid., p. 223.

Conclusion

1. Kristeva refers to the seminal work of the French psychoanalyst André Green, *Le discours vivant* (Paris: P.U.F. 1992), which situates the work of psycho-analysis at the heart of this coalescence of life and language.
2. Kristeva, 'L'autre langue ou traduire le sensible', p. 27.

Bibliography

Complete list of works by Julia Kristeva

Séméiotiké, Recherches pour une sémanalyse (Paris: Seuil 1969).

Le Texte du roman: Approche sémiologique d'une structure discursive transformationelle (The Hague: Mouton 1970).

Des Chinoises (Paris: Editions Des Femmes 1974).

La révolution du langage poétique, L'avant-garde à la fin du XIXème siècle: Lautréamont et Mallarmé (Paris: Seuil 1974).

La Traversée des signes (Paris: Seuil 1975).

Polylogue (Paris: Seuil 1977).

Folle Vérité (Paris: Seuil 1979).

Pouvoirs de l'horreur: Essai sur l'abjection (Paris: Seuil 1980).

Le langage cet inconnu (Paris: Seuil 1981).

Histoires d'amour (Paris: Denoël 1983).

Au commencement était l'amour: Psychanalyse et Foi (Paris: Hachette 1985).

Soleil noir, dépression et mélancolie (Paris: Gallimard 1987).

Etrangers à nous-mêmes (Paris: Fayard 1988).

Les Samouraïs (Paris: Fayard 1990) (novel).

Lettre Ouverte à Harlem Désir (Paris, Rivage 1990).

Le viel homme et les loups (Paris: Fayard 1991) (novel).

Les nouvelles maladies de l'âme (Paris: Fayard 1993).

Le temps sensible, Proust et l'expérience littéraire (Paris: Gallimard 1994).

Sens et non-sens de la révolte: Pouvoirs et limites de la psychanalyse I (Paris: Fayard 1996).

Possessions (Paris: Fayard, 1996) (novel).

La révolte intime: Pouvoirs et limites de la psychanalyse II (Paris: Fayard 1997).

Catherine Clément/Julia Kristeva. *Le féminin et le sacré* (Paris: Stock 1998).

Translations

Revolution in Poetic language, trans. Margaret Waller (New York: Columbia University Press 1984).

About Chinese Women, trans. Anita Barrows (New York and London: Marion Boyars 1977).

Desire in language: A Semiotic Approach to Literature and Art, trans. Thomas S. Gora, Alice Jardine, and Leon S. Roudiez (Oxford: Basil Blackwell 1980).

Powers of Horror: An Essay on Abjection, trans. Leon S. Roudiez (New York: Columbia University Press 1982).

In the Beginning was Love: Psychoanalysis and Faith, trans. Arthur Goldhammer (New York: Columbia University Press 1987).

Tales of Love, trans. Leon S. Roudiez (New York: Columbia University Press 1987).

Black Sun: Depression and Melancholia, trans. Leon S. Roudiez (New York: Columbia University Press 1989).

Language: The Unknown (Brighton: Harvester 1989).

Strangers to Ourselves, trans. Leon S. Roudiez (New York: Columbia University Press 1991).

Nations without Nationalism (New York: Columbia University Press 1993).

The Old Man and the Wolves, trans. Barbara Bray (New York: Columbia University Press 1994).

Proust and the Sense of Time, trans. Stephen Bann (London: Faber and Faber 1993).

New Maladies of the Soul, trans. Leon Roudiez (New York: Columbia University Press 1994).

Time and Sense: Proust and the Experience of Literature, trans. Leon S. Roudiez (New York: Columbia University Press 1996).

Articles, select bibliography

'Un nouveau type d'intellectuel: le dissident', *Tel Quel* 74 (Winter 1977), pp. 3–8.

'Il n'y a pas de maître à langage', *Nouvelle Revue de Psychanalyse* 20 (Autumn 1979), pp. 119–40.

'Les nouvelles maladies de l'âme', *L'Infini* 45 (Spring 1994), pp. 67–73.

'Monstrueuse Intimité (De la littérature comme expérience)', *L'Infini* 48 (Winter 1994), pp. 55–61.

'Bulgarie, ma souffrance', *L'Infini* 49 (Spring 1995), pp. 42–52.

'L'expérience littéraire est-elle encore possible?', *L'Infini* 53 (Spring 1996), pp. 20–46.

'L'autre langue ou traduire le sensible', *L'Infini* 57 (Spring 1997), pp. 15–28.

Suggested Further Reading

Works on Kristeva

Fletcher, John and Andrew Benjamin (eds), *Abjection, Melancholia and Love: The Work of Julia Kristeva* (London: Routledge 1990).

Guberman, Ross (ed.), *Julia Kristeva Interviews* (New York: Columbia University Press 1996).

Lechte, John, *Julia Kristeva* (London: Routledge 1990).

Moi, Toril (ed.), *The Kristeva Reader* (Oxford: Basil Blackwell 1986).

Oliver, Kelly, *Reading Kristeva* (New York: Routledge 1993).

— (ed.), *Ethics, Politics and Difference in Julia Kristeva's Writing* (London: Routledge 1993).

Rose, Jacqueline, 'Julia Kristeva: take two', in Jacqueline Rose, *Sexuality in the Field of Vision* (London: Verso 1996).

Smith, Anna, *Julia Kristeva: Readings of Exile and Estrangement* (London and Basingstoke: Macmillan 1996).

Smith, Anne-Marie (ed.), 'Powers of Transgression/Julia Kristeva', *Paragraph, a Journal of Critical Theory*, 20, no. 3, November 1997 (Edinburgh University Press).

Related Works

Benvenuto, Bice and Roger Kennedy, *The Works of Jacques Lacan: An Introduction* (London: Free Association Books 1986).

Brennan, Teresa, *The Interpretation of the Flesh* (Routledge: London 1995).

Cixous, Hélène and Catherine Clément, *La Jeune Née* (Paris: UGE, 10/18, 1975); *The Newly Born Woman*, trans. Betsy Wing (Minneapolis: University of Minnesota Press 1986).

Feldstein, Richard and Judith Roof (eds), *Feminism and Psychoanalysis* (Ithaca: Cornell University Press 1989).

Laplanche, Jean and Bertrand Pontalis, *Vocabulaire de la psychanalyse* (Paris: Presses Universitaires de France 1967); *The Language of Psychoanalysis*, trans. David Nicholson-Smith (London: Hogarth Press 1973).

Joyce MacDougall, *Eros aux mille et un visages* (Paris: Gallimard 1996); *The Many Faces of Eros* (London, Free Association Books 1995).

Marks, Elaine and Isabelle de Courtivon, *New French Feminisms: An Anthology* (Brighton: Harvester 1981).

Moi, Toril, *Sexual/Textual Politics: Feminist Literary Theory* (London: Methuen 1982).

Spivak, Gayatri, 'French feminism in an international frame', *Yale French Studies*, 62 (1981), pp. 154–84.

Whitford, Margaret, *Luce Irigaray: Philosophy in the Feminine* (London: Routledge 1991).

Wright, Elizabeth, *Psychoanalytic Criticism: Theory in Practice* (London: Methuen 1984).

Index

Abject 24, 29, 30, 32, 33, 38, 39, 46, 88
Abjection 29, 36, 38, 39, 50
Abjection, Melancholia and Love: The Work of Julia Kristeva (1990) 5
Abraham and Torok 39, 46
Affect 22
Agape 34, 51
A la recherche du temps perdu (1909) 66
'L'âme et l'image' (1994) 63
America 7, 35
Aragon, Louis 72, 88
Arendt, Hannah 36, 86, 87, 90
Augustin Saint 95
'L'autre langue ou traduire le sensible'(1997) 80–4

Bann, Stephen 5
Barthes, Roland 65, 72, 73, 74, 88
Baudelaire, Charles 83
Being 63
Berlin wall 77
Britain 7, 35
Bulgaria 12, 77, 80, 82, 83
'Bulgarie, ma souffrance'(1995) 80–3

Cahiers du Grif 86
Catholicism European 11

Catholic theology 65
Chora 60
Cixous, Hélène 9, 11
Contat, Michel 74
Crews, Frederick 8
Critique 4
Cursive time 7

The Dead (1907) James Joyce 24–7
The Dead (1987) John Huston 26–7
Derrida, Jacques 11
'El Desdichado' (1854), Nerval 40–3
Deutsch, Hélène 85
Dissidence 2, 11, 78
Dostoevsky, Fedor 29

'L'enfant au sens indicible'(1993) 58
Eros 34, 51
L'être parlant 17
Etrangers à nous-mêmes (1988) 28, 79–80
'L'étrangeté du phallus' (1996) 71, 88–94
L'Etre 63, 81
Eugénie Grandet (1832), Balzac 45–8, 80
'L'expérience littéraire est-elle encore possible ?' (1996) 85–6, 89–90

Experience 1, 56, 59, 64, 84, 85

Felix Culpa 34
Female homosexuality 37, 45, 61, primary homosexuality 87
'Female sexuality' (1931), Freud 36, 62, 88
Feminine, The 3, 10, 21, 71, 72, 92
Femininity 9, 10, 12, 25, 30–2, 36, 38, 52, 60, 71, 73, 77, 78, 91–4, 97
Feminism, Anglo-American 5, 9, 10, 11; French 9–11. Kristeva's feminism 86
Foreign, The 8
Foreignness 9, 11, 36, 77–83
Fort-da 23, 33
Francblin, Catherine 11
France 2, 7, 8, 9, 11, 13, 77, 78, 82, 83
Freud, Sigmund 7, 36, 50, 55, 61–2, 66, 72, 75, 87, 88, 95
Freudian psychoanalysis 4
Freudian Kristeva 7, 8

Genotext 21
Goya, Francisco 59
Green, André 22, 102
Gross, Elizabeth 35–6

Hegel, Georg 65, 89
Heidegger, Martin 65
Huston, John 26, 27
Hysteria 9, 57–8
Histoires d'amour (1983) 28, 34–5, 44, 49–53, 63

Ignatius de Loyola, Saint 95

Imaginary, The 50, 56, 60, 95
Incorporation 39, 40
L'Infini 54, 60, 64, 85
Institut Charlemagne 59
Introjection 39, 40
Irigaray, Luce 9, 11, 48
'Il n'y a pas de maître à langage' (1994) 91

Jakobson, Roman 65
Jardine, Alice 5, 53
Joyce, James 24–6, 53, 65
Julia Kristeva (1990) 5, 15, 33

Kant, Immanuel 95
Klein, Melanie 18
Kristeva, Julia, biographical detail 2–4, 77
The Kristeva Reader (1986) 5

Lacan, Jacques 15, 60, 62, 87
Lalangue 62
Lautréamont, Comte de 19, 20
Lechte, John 5, 15, 33
Leonardo da Vinci 38
Levi, Primo 96
London 10
Loyola, (*see* Ignatius de Loyola)

Mallarmé, Stéphane 19, 20, 21
The maternal 3, 10, 23, 29, 30–8, 45–8, 50, 79
Maoism 73
Marxism 73
Melancholia 24, 38, 39, 40, 45

Melancholy 30, 39, 40, 41, 42, 44, 79, 88
Merleau-Ponty, Maurice 65, 67, 95
Minoan-Mycenean civilisation 36, 62
Mise en procès 24
Modern European Thinkers 8
Moi, Toril 5
Le Monde 82
Le Monde des Livres 74
'Monstrueuse intimité'(1994) 64–5, **68–9**
Monumental time 7
'Le Mot, le dialogue, le roman'(1967) 4

Nerval, Gérard de 23, 40, 41, 42, 44, 68
'Nerval, El Desdichado' (1983) 40
Nobel symposium, 'Language and Mind' (1994) 64
Les nouvelles maladies de l'âme (1993), 30, 55–8, 61, 63, 68, 85, 87, 90
'Les nouvelles maladies de l'âme', (*L'Infini*) (1994) 11, 54–5
'Un nouveau type d'intellectuel: le dissident' (1977) 11, 78

O'Connor, Noreen 37
Oedipe-bis 71, 91–4
Oedipus complex 91
Oliver, Kelly 5, 53
Ontogenesis 62

Paris 2, 77
Parlêtre 62

Phenotext 21
Pouvoirs de l'horreur **(1980) 17, 28, 30, 33, 35, 44, 63**
Pouvoirs et limites de la psychanalyse **(1997) 4, 38, 84, 86**
Powers of Transgression 10
Phylogenesis 62
Proust, Marcel 38, 43, 59, 64, 65, 66, 67, 69, 75, 76, 78, 88, 89
Psychic bisexuality 38, 93

Rée, Jonathan 73
Rejet 33
La révolution du langage poétique **(1974) 3, 12, 14–23, 30, 63, 66, 76**
La révolte intime **(1997) 30, 84, 86**
Revolt 1, 20, 33, 38, 63, 64, 67, 70, 72–4, 96
Révolte 64
Revolution 19, 21, 24, 29, 33, 50, 67, 70, 72, 83
Rimbaud, Arthur 20
Romance etymology 64
Rose, Jacqueline 68
Roudiez Leon 5
Routledge 35

Sacrifice 36, 90–1
Sallenave, Danielle 85, 89
Sartre, Jean-Paul 72, 73, 74, 88, 89, 95
Semiotic 14–22, 30, 38, 39, 40, 43, 58, 71, 84, 87, 91
Sens 21
Sens et non-sens de la révolte **(1996) 20, 28, 30, 58, 63, 70–2, 74, 86–8, 92**
Sensible, The 20, 38, 65, 92

Sexual identity 11, 24, 37, 53
Signifiance 18
Signification 18, 21
Smith, Anna 5
Smith, Anne-Marie, other relevant publications 10, 27, 41, 45
Soleil noir (1987) 35, 39, 40, 45, 46, 48, 49, 63, 85, 87
Sollers, Philippe 3, 77, 82
Speaking the Unspeakable 96
'Stabat Mater' (Héréthique de l'amour) (1976) 30–2, 84–6
Staël, Mme. de 85
Still, Judith 10
Stone, Jennifer 5, 53
Sujet-en-procès 24
Symbolic 14–22, 38, 39, 40, 43, 50, 55, 58, 70, 73, 84, 88, 91

Symbolic father, The 37, 38, 52

Tel Quel 3, 12, 34, 53, 73, 78
'Le temps des femmes' (1979) 90
Le temps sensible 20, 56, 58, 63, 66–8, 75, 76, 78, 88
Thetic 22
Times Higher Educational Supplement 82
Transference 49–54
Transferential structures 41, 43
Transubstantiation 65
Triolet, Elsa 89

Université de Paris VII 3, 18, 68, 86
University of Warwick 35

Le viel homme et les loups (1991) 34, 59, 77

Printed and bound by CPI Group (UK) Ltd, Croydon, CR0 4YY

09/06/2025

14685867-0004